CAMUS:

Absurd North America

by

Peter Robbins

DORRANCE PUBLISHING CO
EST. 1920
PITTSBURGH, PENNSYLVANIA 15238

Dorrance Publishing Co
585 Alpha Drive
Suite 103
Pittsburgh, PA 15238
Visit our website at *www.dorrancebookstore.com*

ISBN: 978-1-6366-1277-5
eISBN: 978-1-6366-1863-0

— PREFACE —

The presidential election of November 3, 2020, resulted in the defeat of President Donald Trump by Democratic candidate Joe Biden, who received 306 Electoral College votes, the same winning number as Trump got in 2016. However, Trump refuses to concede defeat, claiming, with no evidence, massive fraud in the voting and vote counting. In an unprecedented national turnout, Biden received more than 80 million votes and Trump a little more than 74 million (itself an ominous record). Many Republicans fear that if they try too hard to persuade him do the constitutionally correct thing, he and his now more numerous and more ardent followers will feel betrayed, and refuse to help the GOP win the two Georgia runoff seats needed to stop the Democrats gaining a majority in the U.S. Senate. Trump could be vindictive enough to use his instinctive grasp of "American carnage" — his words in his 2017 inaugural address — to spread more of it, wider and deeper, than he already has during his term in office.

November 23, 2020

The proposed 1/6 commission needs to investigate (a) the Canadian flag going up the Capitol steps as possible evidence of foreign-inspired terrorism and (b) the role of the antler-and-fur-clad "shaman." In video of the alleged insurrection — an impeachable offence but grounds for conviction only in the court of public opinion — Jake Angeli, dubbed the Q-Anon Shaman, seems curiously unrelated to the political slogans shouted, flags waved and insignia worn. He has his mouth open a lot, but roaring rather than speaking. Or was he the divine breath of the insurrectionists' spirituality? Was he channelling the Great Spirit of many North American indigenous peoples? Was the event more than just a epiphany, a magi(c) moment, but also a day of reckoning for aboriginal displacement, dispossession and despoliation?

February 19, 2021

— INTRODUCTION —

Oh, Canada, once again under threat of dismemberment. The 2019 general election delivered a Liberal Party minority government confronted by a Conservative Party official opposition with a popular-vote majority and by a third-party Bloc Québécois that is lukewarm at best about the Canadian federal state. The fourth party, the bouncy New Democratic Party, has enough seats to give the government a majority in a House vote of confidence and, with its party organization in a deep financial hole, does not want another election yet. Three less disparate opposition parties have once before tried ganging up to defeat the government. A poll taken in 2008, at the height of the "prorogation crisis," found that a majority of Canadians, perhaps looking to their American cousins' example, wanted the electorate, not MPs (Members of Parliament), to choose the Prime Minister and his/her government.

Bloc leader Yves-François Blanchet may pedal an eco-friendly bicycle, but the BQ drives a secession bus carrying "soft separatist" passengers, enough of whom (50% +?) may vote for veiled separation in a referendum to end up with the real, naked thing. Since the bowel-scouring 1995 referendum on "sovereignty-association," a poison pill lodged in the confusing question put to Quebeckers by their duplicitous Premier

Jacques Parizeau, they seem to have settled for constitutional monarchy. Which means the little old lady with big hats and funny handbags (or is it funny hats and big handbags that can carry unwanted banquet "treats" home for her corgis?), who speaks French, as their head of state; rather than some rabid Robespierre from Rimouski stomping around the world, at Quebec taxpayer expense, telling the few who care and anybody else within range: "Je suis le Président du Québec and you're not." The accession of Charles III or Guillaume V could move the swingometer against constitutional monarchy. Less so perhaps if we had, say, a naturalized Canadian ex-royal Governor-General who would give us an American actress as Mrs. G-G—a cut or three above Mrs. Simpson. Or we could have a very long-shot Henri IX doing double duty as King of Canada, Australia, New Zealand, England and Wales (Scotland and Northern Ireland would have long left the U.K.) and head of the Commonwealth— "I'm 'eneri IX, je suis, je suis." Or he could be Harold III, the second Anglo-Saxon King, along with his son Archie, Prince of Wales.

The White Palace (called "a dump" by its present royal presence before he moved in) houses a monarchically inclined President Donald I and, ex officio, his heir-apparent Donald II, presently Prince of Wails. What about favourite daughter Ivanka, whom Trump said he wished he was younger for? The speculation about that, which he encourages, is p-p-positively m-m-medieval. Second daughter Tiffany and second son Eric the Unready played bit parts in the RNC chorus of Trump praise but have essentially exeunt this tragicomedy. Which leaves his youngest son, who's already a baron, and his mother, the Slovenian sphinx. Other than his recently deceased brother Robert, the President's siblings (and a niece) have revealed in various ways that they found him to be a very disagreeable family member.

Canada's Tories got their popular-vote majority thanks in large part to winning all but one Alberta riding by massive "surplus vote" numbers—

in some ridings, all other candidates were a combined 10% of also-rans. The enemy (no more merely an adversary) is, as ever, a federal government with a national energy policy/program—sneakier than the last one, but led by the son of a…another Liberal Prime Minister who, along with his Energy minister and fellow francophone intellectual Marc Lalonde, created the first NEP. PM Justin Trudeau used 4.5 billion taxpayer dollars to buy Kinder Morgan's pipeline right-of-way for the transport of Alberta "heavy" oil to tidewater in B.C. An alternative route, down the Mackenzie River valley to Inuvik by the Arctic Ocean's Beaufort Sea, was talked to death by the Berger inquiry (1974-'77). Its report recommended a ten-year delay on the pipeline, which was being proposed for natural gas only; but even then there was heavy-duty opposition from environmentalist opinion, linked to aboriginal land title and usage claims.

As for Canadian unity, the long procedural delays in approving the pipeline have so irritated so many Albertans—across the political spectrum, from true-blue Tory to pink-orange NDP—that some of them have started a western separatist party. Premier Jason Kenney, a federal Tory cabinet minister under PM Stephen Harper and now leader of Alberta's United Conservative Party, is under investigation for alleged dirty tricks against Brian Jean, UCP leadership contender and former leader of the more right-wing and Alberta-first Wild Rose Party. (Any party calling itself "United" is trying to paper over disunity.) Kenney says the "right" things about Alberta being undervalued and mistreated by Ottawa—also saying them in French, for the benefit of Quebec (the other rebel without a cause in Confederation, some say) but not necessarily to his own political benefit as a defender of the West. Some others point out that B.C. is even more West, but that's like saying California is America's West because it has a Pacific coastline. The 2019 election map shows Canada's Tory-blue wall-to-wall starting not many miles east of the coast. Except for two or three orange spots (stains?), it extends all the way through most of B.C. and Alberta and all of Saskatchewan. Manitoba is also a prairie province but, like B.C., regularly elects a patchwork of Liberal, Conservative and NDP MPs. Support for the B.C. (NDP) government's time-consuming, rear-guarding resistance to (tepid) federal and (red-hot) Alberta pressure for the pipeline was heavily concentrated on the coast, less so in Vancouver and its suburbs. Vancouver Island is all Green and NDP, but some of the latter are more industry- than eco-friendly, less so in Vancouver city and its suburbs.

There is a febrile expectation that before the first (diluted) bitumen flows into the hold of the first super-tanker, two not unrelated things will happen: carbon-caused climate change will reach a public-opinion tipping-point; and wild global market fluctuations in supply of and demand for fossil fuels will seriously impair the profitability of their exploration, production and transport. Added to which is the prospect of costly new safety and other regulations. In a pigs-may-fly scenario, Quebec (separated or not) busts sanctions on the purchase of Venezuelan oil; and Alberta breaks its fossil-fuel habit, weaning itself from seven decades of sucking on the oil teat. If it falls further into provincial have-not status, it will be hard to attract U.S. annexation—that was a vector overlooked by St. John's merchants who wanted Newfoundland to join the U.S. not Canada in 1949. Alternatively, Alberta could lead a movement to make one province out of the three westernmost ones. That would make the many prairie retirees who have bought expensive oceanfront properties an intriguing addition to the new province's public opinion and electoral mix. It would also give Ottawa two fewer first ministers to do battle with; and those "eastern bastards" would have a (by then) thirteen-million-person powerhouse partner in Confederation. It could be called SaskATchewan—Canadian cool.

But Premier Kenney is doubling down. Not content with the TMX pipeline underway—with all but no-hope opposition lawsuits dismissed—Alberta and Teck are starting a second, even bigger oil/tar sands production pit north of Fort Mac: the Frontier project. Teck has decided to pull out (for now?) because, Kenney says, of uncertainty about federal carbon-emissions policy. Teck is more circumspect, citing "Indigenous rights," the burgeoning climate change crisis debate and the global oil market. Alberta's appeal court ruled against the federal carbon tax. So, says Premier Kenney, it's all Trudeau's fault. If the Supreme Court of Canada were to rule in favour of federal taxing power over natural resources when mixed with environmental concerns—a complex federal-provincial jurisdiction issue—one wonders (but not for long) what Kenney would say then.

Teck's capitalization of "Indigenous" is of some minor interest—as illustrated below with reference to First Peoples, First Nations and First Governments, spellings that recognize the higher, and equal, status achieved by, and awarded to, aboriginal peoples (now officially Aboriginals or Indigenous). The most-favoured generic in Canada is "aboriginal" (despite its derogatory short form in Australia, "abo.") In the U.S., it's "Native Indian" and not Amerindian, a portmanteau word that refers to the aboriginal peoples of the Americas, North and South—which has the politically loaded connotation that they are all one group, regardless of ethnic and racial mixing, and language and political boundaries imposed upon them. The short-lived American Indian Movement fought federal government policing of aboriginal reserved lands. One of the main aims of Canadian aboriginals, from Mohawk lands in the southeast to Wet'suwet'en lands in the northwest, has been to get the RCMP gendarmerie off their territory—and that included the Canadian Army in the Mohawk case. Most traditional aboriginal lands in the U.S. have long been overrun by non-aboriginal commerce, with varying degrees of aboriginal participation. In Canada, there are

vast tracts of unceded land on which scattered commercial and industrial enterprise is capitalized (in that word's other meaning), owned
and/or operated by non-aboriginal private-sector corporations, but
overseen by tribal or intertribal councils, supported by federal and provincial departments responsible for "aboriginal affairs" (or whatever
they name or rename themselves). U.S. aboriginals have long been the
disregarded by-catch in a federal policy net made by and for non-aboriginals.

In relations between aboriginals and non-aboriginals, the big difference
between the Canadian and American experience has been one of geography and demography. American governments adapted to massive, violent expansionist pressures on a broad front by falling in with a
preference for extermination tempered by enforced assimilation. Like
American governments, British and Canadian ones let land speculation
chicanery, habitat dispossession, starvation and disease solve a lot of the
indigenous "problem." Canadians instituted their own peculiar version
of assimilation: a system of (mostly Anglican-and-Catholic-church-run)
residential schools meant to remould, to varying degrees, Indian, Métis
and Inuit children as Christian European-Canadians. Critics of that system, which is a living memory, can now tell its few remaining defenders
that it looks awfully like the current Chinese government's policy towards Muslim Uighurs in Xinjiang. The Canadian family separation
plan, to take the native out of the natives, has been called cultural genocide. The fact that the planners were not intent on extermination and
that their assimilation plan failed does not invalidate the charge that it
was inhuman and not to be excused on the grounds that racist (or just
racialized?) eugenics was part of then "enlightened" opinion.

The People's Republic of China is now subjecting its Muslim Uighur
people to a kind of collective brainwashing and enforced amnesia; and
razing mosques and other cultural artifacts in an attempt to destroy all

physical evidence of their having been there. It makes the official Han miscegenation policy for Tibetans look positively benign. (However, proselytizing monotheistic religion has always been a threat to Chinese "harmony," starting with the Taiping Rebellion led by a Christian convert.) It would seem that the different kinds of genocide practiced in the 20th century have been not only a dreadful warning but also a source of useful precedents for the "unitarian" brand of authoritarianism. We should be careful about calling anything genocide if it's less than an attempt to exterminate a whole people and/or obliterate its memory. But Canada, with its record of enthusiastic UN participation, has been remarkably insouciant about the danger of being caught in the net of a "crimes against humanity" indictment for treatment of its aboriginal peoples.

· · · · ·

What is presently happening below our southern border is the latest installment of "OMG, what are those crazy Americans up to now?!" The Trump Follies have a faithful Canadian following, some approving of the Donald's (mis)conduct—and some for the same reason as some Americans: hearty dislike of politics as usual in "correct" political disguise. There is another, distinctly Canadian connection. Prime Minister Justin Trudeau, heir to both his father's *savoir faire* and his mother's waywardness, annoys President Trump. While Trump was talking at the press for half an hour, thus delaying his appointed arrival to meet with other world leaders, Trudeau was caught making disparaging comments about Trump, in French to Emmanuel Macron and in English to Boris Johnson, who fancies himself an English (more humorous) version of Trump. Video footage shows neither man amused by Trudeau's attempt at comic relief. But being made fun of, however mildly, angers Trump; doing it fluently in two languages is bound to enrage him.

This book is not about politics so much as about Canadian and American political speech, about political language, its usage and abusage. My computer has accepted that last word, even though the OED doesn't—but then Word is an American word-processing program. Americans have always been more welcoming of novelty than Canadians, whose old and fading British connection means that some of them write labour, not labor, and centre, not center, and some all four, depending on what they're writing and for whom. My computer redlines labour but not centre. I guess Americans don't care about spelling consistency. Why not go the whole Shavian hog: nayber, lite, xtra…? The OED accepts the second as a generic, thanks to relentless advertising of food and drink labelled Lite because it's supposed to be better for you. And it recognizes U.S. (sorry, US) spelling. The biggest difference is hyphen usage (hyphenage?). But you don't want to get hung up, because mobile-phone texting has opened the floodgates 4 U. Mobile phone texting (or mobile phone-texting) could be about the texter moving around. Using a term favoured by some historians of the closely woven Canadian-American relationship, this book is "transnational"—or cross-cultural, and not, it is hoped, too cross (ly) or crass (ly) cultural.

The eruption of Donald Trump onto the American presidential (and world) stage has brought some disturbingly strange mannerisms into political speech. President Putin's denial of Russian interference in U.S. elections was "powerful." Of course it was, having been said by one power-tripper alone with another. But was it credible? Godlike fisher of folk, Trump confidently predicts a big success before he has even put his line in the water, adding "It'll be so big you won't believe it" or "It'll be so great you'll ask me to stop" (or words to that effect). Those are safe predictions, Mr. President, no matter what you say is in your net or that you're going to do or put on the American kitchen table. Trump's overuse of the word "incredible" defies—and destroys—belief.

Everyday conversational use of the word to mean amazing or wonderful has been contaminated by his turning it into a rhetorical device. When his promises are belied by facts, events and sworn testimony, he simply changes his story. Or, as is increasingly his habit, he repeats the same old falsehood often enough that almost half the country believes him and the rest admit defeat by exhaustion. Or his handlers—a misnomer; nobody can handle Trump—produce "alternative facts" in support of their master. His favourite escape route is: "We'll see what happens"— when there's doubt and a credibility issue, which there always is and nowhere more so than with any Trump utterance or initiative.

Trump observers have often noted what they call deflection and distraction in his and his surrogates' answers to what they regard as unfriendly questions. They also use what might or might not be a deliberate strategy of confusion. As a (former) Hansard editor of the official report of debates in British Columbia's legislative assembly, I heard some opposition critics of a government bill or motion use what sounded like a haphazard, hastily assembled wall of words. Were they trying to impede government attempts to clarify or just make its case? Or were they simply in character, speaking as they always did in heated debate? It's a catchy technique. Is it innate or is it contagious, or both? Some Trump spokespeople have been using it ever since he declared his candidacy. In House debate on impeachment articles, Congressman Doug Collins was a masterly practitioner, speaking very fast, barely drawing breath, and throwing together what sounded like sentence fragments. It's the Sarah Palin legacy—something that Trump can finally thank John McCain for.

If the audio of a Collins retort were slowed down, it might make better sense for a listener; on the other hand, it might have the effect of making him sound impaired, which was the intended result of a "doctored" version of a Nancy Pelosi statement. We now have technologically sophisticated "deep fakes" of not just the words but also the facial expressions, even facial structure, of people, especially prominent or celebrity persons. This kind of thing may remind Canadians of a 1993 Tory election ad that photo-shopped a picture of Liberal leader Jean Chrétien. The left side of his face, damaged by childhood Bell's palsy, was highlighted, making him look, say aficionados of this kind of thing, like the getaway driver in a French gangster flick. It did the Kim Campbell (Canada's first, and very short-lived, female Prime Minister) campaign no good, although she may have played no part in the ad's making.

At this writing, Trump is on trial before the U.S. Senate for impeachable offences as determined by the House of Representatives. He is an odds-on favourite to be acquitted by a fearful Senate Republican majority. And unless the Democratic Party unites in support of one "safe," moderate presidential nominee—neither Sen. Amy Klobuchar nor Mayor Pete (women and gays having been deemed unelectable), but former Vice-President Joe Biden Jr., Trump's worst fear unless he can be smeared by son Hunter Biden's alleged Ukrainian misdeeds—President Donald J. Trump will probably be re-elected. One of Trump's two alleged offences is also about Ukraine and its reputation for egregious political and economic corruption. In a phone call to the newly elected President Zelensky he linked a "favour"—Zelensky to announce an investigation into the Bidens, father and son, for their role in Ukraine's energy finance—to the release of congressionally approved military aid to the Ukrainians, aid which Trump claimed he was withholding absent a Ukrainian clean bill of health.

Broken News from CNN: Trump has been acquitted, although one GOP Senator voted for his removal from office, for one of the two offences for which he had been impeached. He examined the evidence as presented by Democratic members of the House intelligence and judiciary committees and used his common sense. Of no small interest is the fact that that one Senator, Mitt Romney, is a Mormon. Which means his faith commands him to believe that absolute religious truth was written on tablets dug up by Joe Smith, in 1830 in his back garden, as he was ordered to do by an angel named Moroni. Any temptation to mock Mormonism can be quashed by reading *Educated*, a memoir by Tara Westover. It's a harrowing tale of an upbringing in a large, super-fundamentalist Mormon family in Buck's Peak, Idaho, one ruled by a father regularly disappointed when the world of science and government, and the Illuminati who secretly run it, were not destroyed by the apocalypse foretold in the sacred text he continually read and reread, out loud for all to hear. She and three of her brothers managed to tear themselves away, and into the damnation of "gentile" life. As a child, she was expected to help both her father in his scrap-metal business (which meant hard physical labour) and her mother, who was a herbalist in "God's pharmacy." As a girl (a "wench") and then a young woman (a "whore"), to leave the fold took extraordinary courage and will power. One of her brothers seems to have been more than just his father's son, a bipolarity sufferer, but also some sort of psychopath—his attempts to prevent her escape from the gulag were often physically violent. Romney (who is not Father Westover) used his faith—and "used" is a word used against him by those questioning his honesty—to help him conclude that what must have been obvious to his craven colleagues should be said and voted accordingly. Of course, Romney is on Trump's enemies list. Is he being shunned by his fellow Republicans because he made them look so bad?

Trump is his own worst enemy. Who else would say that a phone call was "perfect"? All he needed to say was that there was nothing wrong with it. Anyone who says, with conviction, "I'm a stable genius" and "I know more about war than my(?) generals," declares himself mentally unfit for high (or any other) office. Perhaps he was elected because, apart from his 2016 opponent being regarded as a political dominatrix, he made people laugh. At his exaggerations? At the insults and jejune nicknames he lobs at his opponents and critics? Maybe people voted him to be the first entertainment President. He badly wants his pseudo-presidential reality TV show to be more popular than President Obama singing "Amazing Grace."

— CHAPTER 1 —

Political Constitutions and Cultures

Peter Russell has described the history of Canada as one of three "pillars" built on "incomplete conquests." The longest and strongest pillar was the British imperial connection—economically, politically, legally and culturally. The second was and still is the French *canadien* fact; and the third is now the aboriginal or First Peoples factor. They are also called First Nations, and call themselves First Governments when negotiating land claims with federal and provincial governments. Canadians with strong ancestral connections to the "mother country" Britain forget about the contribution that North American Indians made to Canada not becoming part of the United States in that country's first fragile but feisty decades. They remember Laura Secord, a sentimental favourite, more than they do Joseph Brant, leader of Six Nations forces. French-Canadians lost their mother country in 1759, and Quebec became their home and native land well before Confederation in 1867. Long after, they were still being made to feel like subjects rather than citizens by Anglos, a bit like aboriginals' treatment by a long line of federal and provincial governments.

The idea of Canada as a multicultural mosaic grew out of immigration from, first, northwestern Europe, then southern and eastern Europe, and then Asia, the Afro-Caribbean and Africa itself. An interesting feature of this latest wave is the number of people from countries that were once members of the British Empire—they find nothing odd about taking an oath of allegiance to the Queen of Canada. When they discover that Canada is more than multicultural, multi-ethnic and multiracial, it's multinational, they may be less sure about what they've come to— about where they have travelled in psychic time as well as physical space. Pierre Trudeau's 1982 "patriation" of the Canadian constitution severed the last umbilical cord, appeal to Britain's Privy Council. His second, companion initiative, the Charter of Rights and Freedoms, influenced by the U.S. Bill of Rights (amendments to their constitution), produced a revitalized Supreme Court. The Constitution Act, 1982, supersedes the British North America Act (renamed Constitution Act, 1867); it and Prime Minister John Diefenbaker's 1960 Bill of Rights remain on the statute books.

One of the (some would say) revolutionary things done by the Supreme Court was recognizing an aboriginal "interest" in constitutional decision-making, followed by recognition of claims to legal title on ancestral lands and, further, of oral history and cultural artifacts as admissible evidence. A recent addition to this sequence is the Tsilhqot'in (Chilcotin) decision, which says that claims to "unceded" land based on "immemorial" usage—often supported by archaeological "finds"—are justiciable. Private property owners and developers of such lands have found it unprofitable to pursue their claims on those lands in court, even when they have purchase proof of ownership and municipal zoning approval. What sticks in the craw of many of them is that both their compensation (if any) and aboriginals' legal costs are paid by non-aboriginal taxpayers. One foundation for all this is the Royal Proclamation of 1763, guaranteeing protection of Indian lands—how and for how long was, to say the least, uncertain, with American colonial governors in league with land sharks and agents like Daniel Boone, boyish exemplar of Ulster-style "immigration." The proclamation applied to all of British North America, as it then was; the American Revolution ended its application to what became U.S. lands. It is still invoked by Canadian aboriginals. Section 35 of 1982's addition to Canadian constitutionalism guarantees aboriginals' treaty rights; but interpretation of pre-modern treaties is a very time-consuming court(s) process. The Charter does not directly address aboriginals' land claims.

They have learned (partly because they were force-fed the English three Rs in those infamous residential schools) to play the honkies' games—not just ice hockey and football (American and Canadian, as with "Indian" Jack Jacobs of the Green Bay Packers and the Winnipeg Blue Bombers) but also litigation and politics. Most of them live in unhealthy housing on unproductive land. Some have lifted themselves into higher education and relative prosperity; others have taken advantage of federal grants to partake in their tribe's progress; and some chiefs have pilfered federal moneys for their own and "first family" gain. Tribal councils and hereditary chiefdom remain a mystery for most white folk, even as they know less about "their" government than do Indian lawyers and leaders. The SNC-Lavalin—Jody Wilson-Raybould affair exposed Justin Trudeau to the charge that his aboriginal Attorney-General understood constitutional limits on political power better than the Prime Minister's Office (PMO) did. Although some felt that her resistance to the PMO was a bit self-righteous, she stood her ground well, resigning and taking another female member of the cabinet with her—not to mention both the PM's closest political friend and adviser and the Clerk of the Privy Council, top federal civil servant—followed by her re-election (as an Independent) in Vancouver-Granville. She concluded defence of her refusal to allow SNC-Lavalin a deferred prosecution, acting on the advice of her director of public prosecutions, with a proposal that Canada separate the positions of A-G and Minister of Justice, and remove the former from the (always partisan to some degree) cabinet decision-making process, which the U.K. did several years ago.

What a throwback!—to the 18th century and the laying of Canada's foundation on a marriage of convenience between aboriginal peoples and the British Crown. It looks a bit like a renewed alliance: aboriginal assertion of natural justice getting in bed with evolving traditions of British constitutionalism and parliamentary democracy.

· · · · ·

Ambiguity, evasion and obfuscation adhere to all major political concept words. One of the worst offenders in this respect is sovereignty. One sovereignty theorist of note, F.H. Hinsley, says it's "a concept which men in certain circumstances have applied—a quality they have attributed or a claim they have counterposed—to the political power which they or other men were exercising." It should be added that the phrase "in certain circumstances" doesn't mean that they can only be of one kind or set for sovereignty to apply. U.S. A-G Barr recently let slip the word "sovereigns" (plural) in defence of his sending Portland, Oregon, the (unrequested) help of heavily armed forces (wearing iron-on "Police" badges) to quell riotous protests—as an additional benefit of their stated mission, protection of federal buildings. Shared sovereignty is the apotheosis of a political concept: its use entails more politicking than, say, power, authority and constitutionality, even natural rights and social justice. That's because it seems an obvious contradiction in terms—which is why so many Canadian academics say that Canadian federalism is impossible but so far, so good. (Isn't that what the jokey little moron said as he fell past the seventeenth floor?) Not that Canada is unique in its federal and provincial (dual) departments of agriculture, finance, health, etc., etc. Constitutional lines have been drawn, and experienced ministers and their deputies know how to mutually abide by them and avoid wasteful conflict. However, issues arise (at regular intervals) from the inevitably partisan cabinet decision-making that requires lengthy, head-banging intergovernmental discussion before their resolution, ones needing more than a Zoom conference. U.S. state Governors convening about common concerns doesn't seem to occasion as much ganging up on the feds as do most gatherings of Canada's provincial Premiers. Two possible explanations are: 50 states compared to 10 provinces, one of which has been officially recognized as a nation possessing a kind of exceptional sovereignty (*maîtres chez nous*)—acting like a fully sovereign state if not a nation-state has been an aspect of provincial participation in Canadian federalism from its beginnings. A third one is that at least two of them enjoy disproportionate fiscal power (2-3 of 10 provinces compared to 3-4 of 50 states).

Some say politics is all about the unexpected, or as former U.K. Prime Minister Harold Macmillan wearily replied to an eager journalist's inquiry: "Events, dear boy, events." The ship of state can be knocked off course, severely damaged or even capsized by howling "winds [or waves] of change" coming from unusual quarters or in unforeseen combination; and a truly conservative statesman is at the helm and ready to trim sails. President Trump is one of the "idiotes" that classical Athenian democrats had to deal with. They had made their job easier for themselves by excluding women and slaves. But they were compelled to listen to men who refused to listen to anyone else and paid no attention to what was going on around them; they were blinkered by tunnel vision—at the end of the Trump tunnel is a mirror. One event whose prospect Canadians fear with a blend of horror and fascination is a first ministers' conference or "summit." The sherpas (provincial ministers, their deputies and associated civil servants) getting together tends to be boringly productive of advance to renewed or fresh agreement on how to divide up the fiscal pie—unless the amounts are so big (such as support for health care and post-secondary education) that the big guns get involved. Their meetings to amend, or create new, fiscal arrangements acts are reliably contentious. But squeaky wheels can usually be greased by judicious federal revenue-sharing.

The worst sort of first ministers' meeting is a constitutional amendment meeting. PM Mulroney's Meech Lake and Charlottetown accords made a mockery of the word "accord" (in both official languages). A repeat performance is to be avoided like the plague. To quote another disillusioned but persistently upbeat Brit PM, Winston Churchill, we "keep buggering on." The first question asked by any Canadian PM when confronted by a decision that only he or she can make—and has to answer after what might be nail-biting delay—is: "What will this mean for Canadian unity?" Post-election western storm clouds made Trudeau rush his Deputy Prime Minister and Mrs. Fix-it out to Alberta, where she was born, to start mending fences. Which prompts jokes about Texan hats and cattle, ranges and ranches (many of Alberta's replaced by oil rigs, and many of them now "orphans" needing "remediation"), and the not so funny struggle of some ranchers against fracking's "slick water."

Two well-worn slippery words are responsibility and spirituality. The first has been overtaken by accountability, partly because it asks for an accounting—just the facts, in a full report of what was done (or failed to be done). Responsibility tends to invite a multi-directional conversation—another slippery word—about who as well as what and why. Will it be a friendly chat, one that elicits the truth by lulling the responsible one into inadvertently revealing it? Will it be an exchange of response and retort, and escalate into confrontation, which might provoke a challenge—a daring confession? (The second happens frequently with Trump.) Governments like to delegate, even devolve, responsibility because that sounds more democratic—a version of power going back to the people. Quite apart from responsibilities being transferred without the means of fulfilling them, there's a tacit assumption that their transfer somehow includes responsibility for the act of transfer: "We gave them what they wanted, more responsibility. They asked for it" (this last a kind of *double entendre*). Devolving responsibility should not be seen as an act of giving, or charity, and something it would be "inappropriate" to question.

Spirituality is a quite different case, shrouded in mysticism and New Age rebellion against evidence arrived at by common-sense inference or through lessons learned from scientific method. This frame of mind may include a fondness for conspiracy theories that deny generally accepted facts, one which whispers in your inner ear: "You've been conned by self-appointed experts."

A political example of the first—its adjunct (additional junk) conspiracy theory will be discussed shortly—is tortuous denial of President Trump's so-called quid pro quo. It centers on (a) denying any significance in the immediate juxtaposition of the quid and the quo in his "perfect" phone call to President Zelensky; (b) ignoring the conditional "though" before the quid favour request is dealt; and (c) a late entry, insisting that the "us" for whom a favour is asked is the grammatically (and politically) correct "we the American people" and not the royal "we" (which fits both Trump's enormous ego and the U.S. election of a once and future king every four years). Republican defence of Donald Trump forgets an old GOP mantra: if it walks like a duck and quacks like a duck, it's probably a duck. Trump's Senate trial has forced some of his defenders to acknowledge the error of his ways. They then argue that what he did is less than an impeachable offence under the constitution, and that the commission of some crime must be included in articles of impeachment for them to succeed, at the same time arguing that a sitting President cannot be indicted, which means that he can only be censured for his misconduct because the final stage of impeach-ment, removal from office, is a sentence to punish criminality (proven against President Nixon, who abetted a statutory crime but resigned when it was clear he was going to be impeached). The House can say that Trump's conduct helps define "high crimes and misdemeanors"; but then the Senate can, and did, render a contrary verdict without ap-peal. A good argument for acquittal is a "purely" political one that to convict him when a presidential election is gestating would further in-flame his supporters' belief that the whole process was, in his words, a witch-hunt. Inverting the argument, the passions he has stoked have created a virtual civil war—which could become actual and, as com-mander-in-chief, he would declare martial law. So whether guilty and/or not guilty, Trump would win, a perfect trifecta.

The favour Trump asked of Zelensky was public announcement of an investigation of two prominent American citizens, one of whom was ap-pointed a member of the board of directors of a notoriously corrupt Uk-rainian energy company, the other a U.S. Vice-President who helped arrange his son's appointment and was now seeking the Democratic Party's presidential nomination for the 2020 election. Trump's defenders insisted, against a lot of contrary evidence, that his abiding concern was corruption in Ukraine—and not wanting to pour good U.S. money after bad—rather than the Bidens' involvement in it. It became increasingly apparent that all he really wanted was announcement of an investigation of the Bidens (whom he could have asked "his" A-G to look into much earlier, rather than try cheat-wheedling a foreign government's involve-ment). A supposedly independent Zelensky announcement would have had the effect of smearing Biden long before the investigation issued any findings or report, if it ever even started proceedings.

The conspiracy theory associated with the Ukrainian corruption meme was a thoroughly debunked allegation that it was Ukraine that interfered in the 2016 U.S. election, not Russia. American counter-intelligence services found no evidence that any foreign entity other than the Russian GRU (or some other agency acting for it) cyber-attacked American election advertising and systems. Trump's response was the irrelevant argument that Russian interference did not preclude the possibility of other countries (or 400-pound hacker geeks in their mother's basement) doing it.

Prof. Alan Dershowitz, speaking at Trump's trial in conjunction with his defence counsel, argued that the Framers, in pursuit of the checks and balances of a separation of powers, rejected the British kind of parliamentary democracy (which Hamilton thought they should seriously consider). Under the Westminster model, the executive branch being part of the legislative branch ensures "state capacity" (Francis Fukuyama's words in *Political Order and Political Decay*), meaning more effective power. It also makes the Prime Minister a creature of the "people's house" (House of Commons or, maybe someday, U.S. House of Representatives). A Prime Minister can be ousted from office if a majority of his/her party caucus thinks he/she has to go before any more damage is done, either to the party or the public interest (which, of course, they think are the same thing). A parliamentary vote is a quick and effective way of dealing with perceived (thus damaging even if unproven) misconduct—or even persistent maladministration. A restive back bench dependent on continuing constituency or electoral district support is a more democratic judge and jury than a PM or President claiming that his/her continuation in office is in the greatest public interest—a common political delusion that the diverting Dershowitz endorsed. The foot soldiers of a governing party are in close contact with reporters and other political observers, and with opposition members of their House. That gives them additional insight into public sentiment as well as the benefit of a wide range of opinion. Members of Parliament are ambitious for appointments at their leader's discretion, too; but the leader needs their grass-roots input. They and their leader are interdependent, as were U.S. Congress persons and the President not that long ago. Pictures of President Trump paying a visit to Capitol Hill, and of Senators snuggling up to him with adoring looks, resemble a medieval royal progress. Too many Americans who should know better seem to think that dumping a President is a kind of lèse majesté. Other, stable republics have a separate head of state.

We have now moved on from the impeachment-and-trial drama to a nation at war with Covid-19, the "Chinese virus." After downplaying the novo-corona threat for almost two months, Trump began praising his own prescience—and, of course, his administration's efforts to protect the American people; V-P Mike Pence is trotted out to sprinkle his ever-redundant contributions with "as directed by the President." Prescience is an interesting word in the context of front-line soldiers in this war being unable to access allegedly abundant protective and testing gear, and weary public-health experts repeating (for the umpteenth time) that the U.S. is still behind the curve of this pandemic. The inclusion of some said experts on the podium along with the usual White House crowd, and their being allowed to answer questions (their answers undercut by the President's confusing if not contradictory additions), has not altered the fact that Trump is both pre-science and prehistoric. He can't seem to stop persistently mangling both history and science—to such an extent that daily Covid briefings were suspended. Could talk of a war presidency be a prelude to declaration of a national emergency of such scope that, as commander-in-chief, he postpones November's election until further notification?

PM Trudeau was able—for an unimpeachable reason, his wife's positive Covid-19 test result—to step outside his house to deliver a daily (brief) press briefing that concluded with a bland but undoubtedly heartfelt: "We'll get through this together." The heavy lifting has been left to a panel of cabinet ministers and assorted experts, led by his super-positional Deputy PM, who, unlike President Trump, has faced relatively friendly press probes. Trump seems to feel he has to be there to "correct"—i.e., put a garbled gloss on—whatever his experts say; he seems unable to help himself by just standing aside (looming in his case), a silent symbol of authority.

At this further writing, Trump has abandoned the fight against Covid-19 and hitched his wagon to the fading star of resurgent prosperity. His faithful followers are energized by a vision of "normal" consumer binging unfettered by surgical masks, social distancing and other proven anti-viral measures. This focus shift is abetted by presidential pressure on Governors and public education officials to open schools to full in-person attendance, replacing child care with parental participation in the labour market—all of it a perverse Trumpian version of federal pandemic aid to states—and on drug companies to hurry "warp speed" vaccine development, abridging tests and trials. Fate and the gods (who always punish hubris) have delivered a third whammy to Trump: persistent, endemic police brutality against Afro- and other Americans of colour has lanced the deep, long-festering abscess of racism, adding to the plummet of his opinion poll numbers. He continues to bark "Law and Order." But will voters bite? Only, it seems, Aunt Jemima, Uncle Ben and the whole white-bread band of memorabilians still living on a *Gone With the Wind* movie set.

As for Trudeau, he seems to have stumbled into a hole of his own making and/or the PMO failed to administer the smell test to a proposed multimillion-dollar federal grant for a charity named WE (Oui *en français?*) to put students to worthy work in support of anti-pandemic measures. WE paid some members of his family (and of his Finance minister's) to speak at or otherwise participate in (including travel to) its promotional events and other activities. Fortuitously for Trudeau, stiffing the other two amigos meeting in D.C. on July 8 to celebrate USMCA allowed him to escape embarrassing conflict-of-interest questions from the world's reporters at that event.

· · · · ·

As for rejection of methods, deductive or inductive, that have enjoyed success in establishing facts and systems of knowledge, those who repudiate their use, even when supported by a wide range of experts in relevant fields, can point to notorious cases in which repeated mistakes by some expert witness have been exposed. The remedy is investigation, correction and sworn rebuttal by panels of other experts, not rejection of all professional experts. Conspiracy buffs argue that all experts are part of a plot to deceive non-experts. The only trustworthy approach, say the deniers of anything elite experts say, is true belief in whatever people you like, because they're like you, believe is true. This is what some might call a virtuous circle. Others might call it something less flattering.

The notion of spirituality has achieved wide circulation. Leaving aside the doctrine of spiritualism and communication with spirits of the dead— i.e., those who have passed on (to only they know where)—contemporary spirituality emphasizes a felt connection with a natural environment or social structure that is animated, meaning it has *anima*, as in the Latin for soul(s). Being animated is more than being lively; it's about having a spiritual dimension as well as material dimensions. Spirituality can be about a collective soul at the core of any group of people's consciousness of their way of life in a particular place with a particular set of customs and beliefs. It helps sustain religious and other sects living off the urban and suburban grid, or people floating from one fellowship attachment to another. Such a semi-detached existence is attracted to stories from surviving and remnant indigenous communities, whose inhabitants are classified by anthropologists and ethnologists as animists—insofar as they treat other animals, and plants, as fellow sharers in a world of spirits that must be appeased. Many of the above-mentioned attributes have been adopted and cultivated by non-indigenous "tribes." Professionals working on and with aboriginal peoples have generalized their understanding of aboriginals' experience, and helped spread and inculcate the concept of spirituality among non-aboriginals. It has become an academic category and then a bureaucratic tool in what the Canadian government now calls Crown—Indigenous Relations. The concept of spirituality is behind the use of the term "cultural modification" to help legitimize what might otherwise be considered regrettable, such as some aboriginal peoples' traditional selective stripping of bark from trees for clothing and building purposes or their use of high-tech nets in salmon-spawning rivers.

It is also used in regular, everyday conversation, and in explaining and defending attitudes being questioned on their practical effects and implications. An outgrowth of "spirituality" is "mindfulness," which is more than being thoughtful; it means identifying with others. It's partly based on the super-confessional J.-J. Rousseau's writings about innate fellow-feeling and education of the moral sentiments. I once heard a youngish mother asking her very young son, who kept throwing a stick down a park path, to be more mindful of other people. Okay, I'm a verifiable (or should that be certifiable?) old curmudgeon, but "in my day" the parental reaction would probably have been along the lines of telling the kid to stop, put the stick down, and think about the consequences of his actions: "You might hit somebody." Brat replies: "I don't care." Mother (or father): "I'll make you care" or maybe "How would you like it if they threw it back and it hit you?" Up-to-date brat: "That would be child abuse." If not well before this exchange, patience ends and the brat is, as it were, taken in hand. What intrigued me was her saying "mindful." This is pure New Age thinking and lingo. The kid has probably been inducted into it. Perhaps, *à la* Rousseau, the feeling, the thought, even the word have been educed from him.

— CHAPTER 2 —

Indiscreet Disclosures

At 1:30 a.m. on July 6, 2013, a runaway 74-car fleet of Montreal, Maine and Atlantic Railway oil tankers exploded in the centre of Lac-Mégantic, destroying the centre of this Quebec town and killing 47 people. MMA chairman of the board Ed Burkhardt told stunned survivors that if MMA were to spend more on safety—as in more man-hours of inspection—it would not be competitive in the market for rail transport of dangerous goods. At least he didn't issue a routine statement containing robotic words about MMA's "continuing commitment" to public health, safety and other "community values." Lac-Mégantic was a relatively minor event (for number of casualties) in a litany of mass death, maiming and disease resulting from—and explained away, with crocodile tears, as the price that has to be paid for—adherence to the imperative of corporate profits, consumer savings and shareholder dividends. The worst such events—e.g., the chlorine gas leak in Bhopal, India, and the garment factory collapse in Dhaka, Bangladesh—occur in countries whose safety and other regulations are even laxer than those of "advanced" Western democracies, whose firms firmly disown their distant responsibilities.

. . . . .

Early in his presidency, Trump staged an airport photo op of the return of three haggard Korean-American hostages in which he publicly thanked North Korean dictator Kim Jong-un for being "excellent to them." Two fruitless "summit" meetings in Singapore and Hanoi and a meaningless do-se-do on the Korean DMZ have not dampened Trump's unrequited love affair with the maleficent Kim.

He implicitly asked Russia, on live TV in front of a cheering crowd, to intervene in his favour in the 2016 election: "Russia, if you're listening, I hope you can find those missing 30,000 [former Secretary of State and Democratic Party presidential candidate Hillary Clinton] emails." Evidence that Russia acceded to his request he denies presumably, but in his case improbably, on the grounds that no rational person encourages conduct that could give rise to his criminal prosecution. This includes publicly (as recorded in the Oval Office) telling the Russian Ambassador Sergey Kislyak and the Russian Federation's Minister of Foreign Affairs Sergey Lavrov: "I just fired the head of the FBI. He was crazy, a real nut job. I faced great pressure because of Russia. That's taken off"—and it did indeed take off, to Trump's chagrin. He also told the world that if he shot somebody on Fifth Avenue in broad daylight, he'd get away with it. Many now see his divine-right conduct as the presidential norm. Those who bet their livelihoods, if not their very souls, on his electoral success are compelled to devote less time and energy to advice or counsel and more to polishing the emperor's image and trying to silence those who say he has no clothes. The truth is he doesn't want advice. It would seem he's content to let government look after itself, or not, as best it can, without any coherent policy direction from him—it's the President-c[ompan]y, just like Trump Inc. He has found out he can use the authority of his office to fire whistle-blowing bureaucrats at will.

Why does Trump obsess about Norway as an ideal source of immigrants? Why would Norwegians, living in the most prosperous per capita of all NATO member states, want to emigrate to the U.S.? Why, when asked if he'd accept "dirt" on a political opponent from a foreign source, did he say: "I'd listen if I got a call from, say, Norway"? He has an admitted phobia about alien germs. But does he secretly lust for Henry Miller's Tropics and "hot" people? Does his backroom Rasputin and racist *doppelgänger*, Steven Miller, encourage such fantasies? More "weird shit"—to quote a former President's reaction to Trump's inaugural address.

· · · · ·

If anyone thinks an examination of North American political speech should be less fixated on Trump-speak—unavoidably insofar as he seems to suffer from a bad case of logorrhea—here are some gems from Canada's political elite. One of Canada's few entries in *The Oxford Dictionary of Quotations* comes from Liberal Prime Minister Mackenzie King, who summed up a House of Commons debate on WWII military conscription with this: "Not necessarily conscription, but conscription if necessary." It sounds a little less self-defeating the other way round, but it's classic political evasion of a difficult decision. What actually happened as a result of the debate was enough to satisfy Churchill and Roosevelt's demand for more Canadian troops—made at the 1943 Quebec Conference, and it took some of the shine off the event for its obsequious host. Many volunteers had already been in England awaiting the call to action, which came with the disastrous Dieppe raid shortly after PM King's 1942 speech. His eventual decision was to help out the Allies in the Pacific theatre by putting together a new army, which was finally ready to go west when it was obvious there was no further threat of a Japanese invasion. As his diaries reveal, King regularly consulted his dead mother and his dead dog. He rationalized some morally and politically dubious decisions by appealing to a spiritual posterity in which his mother and pets figured prominently. He came across as one of those seemingly asexual politicians for whom politicking is a kind of sublimation.

Battle-cries are very important for rallying volunteers and voters in election campaigns. In 1972 the Liberal Party of Canada chose to fight for re-election as government under the slogan "The Land is Strong." They could just as well have said "The Sun is Hot" for all the button-pushing effect they got: puzzled indifference. They survived with a minority government needing NDP support. Compare the Democratic Party's 2012 slogan, "Forward!" This single word, meaningless in itself because it has no compass, was supposed to incite people to political action. The Democrats' choice, with its European socialist history (e.g., the left-wing journal *Vorwärts*), could be seen as ironic validation of a favourite Republican accusation.

Be careful, Bernie; but you say you're a *democratic* socialist; and you would probably like to be seen as more like the Canadian NDP than some European neo-Marxian social-democrat party. I know you know about Tommy Douglas, "father of Canadian medicare"; you should talk to his grandson, Kiefer Sutherland, about what you seem not to know about the mixed reality of our publicly funded medicare system. You often refer to your trips north of the border for pensioners' cheaper drugs. But different provinces have different pharmacare thresholds, there is no denticare, and a growing list of so-called extended benefits (ambulance, eyeglasses and hearing-aids, podiatry, physiotherapy, prosthetics, chiropractic, naturopathy, acupuncture, and so on and so on). For many, all this is part of private insurance plans, from Manulife to Green Shield, with various and variable public coverage for prescription drug, health care payment and visit number amounts. Almost all dental work is carried by private insurance, often attached to pension plans;

and it's user-pay (sliding-scale amounts) for procedures not covered. For astronomically expensive drugs developed by big pharma to relieve (not cure) chronic disabling conditions, there's political protest and lobbying, and crowd-funding. Their cost, along with overused lab tests and high-tech scanning, could break the back of our single-payer system, even as it's backstopped by the Canada Health Act, which manages to work well for most Canadians—"guided by" five basic principles: comprehensiveness, universality, portability (in Canada), accessibility and public administration.

• • • • •

The following are some examples of careless talk and, some might say, verbal abuse in the B.C. legislature, culled from an earlier, unreconstructed era in B.C.'s political "conversation"—to call them debate is a bit of a stretch. Interjections are supposed to be reported only if the recognized speaker responds to them—a rule of mixed value, because even if a member who has the floor says nothing in direct response, interjection(s) may have a noticeable effect on his or others' subsequent remarks. The classic case in B.C.'s House is Social Credit Minister of Forests Dave Parker's sole contribution to a debate in which Colin Gabelmann (future NDP A-G) was imploring the government to make sexual orientation a prohibited basis for discrimination under the province's Human Rights Act. Gabelmann was close to tears over what he saw as government obduracy. He was interrupted by Parker growling: "The NDP theme song, Sodomy Forever." All that was heard in response was a collective jaw dropping. No one collected her/himself sufficiently to initiate an intervention. The Hansard jaw dropped, too, but we decided not to insert the style line Interjection—reserved for occasions when what exactly was said is unrecorded but there is a verbal reaction. Gabelmann soldiered on, either stunned or unwilling to dignify Parker's comment with a reply. It could be said that Hansard dropped more than its jaw. While Parker's microphone was not on, the ambient-sound mic picked up enough for the gist of his words to be heard, and there was no doubt in the mind of anyone within earshot about who said them. "Anyone" included most of Parker's colleagues, who prevailed upon him to stand up at the next sitting of the House and "apologize for whatever it is I am supposed to have said."

The old B.C. Hansard sound system picked up fragments of background chatter, muttered conversations and not-so-*sotto-voce* catcalls by members within range of the pre-unidirectional microphone of a member on his or her feet and speaking. One result was that members might share with a wider audience such comments as: "Paddle your black ass back to Jamaica." Rosemary Brown, target of this taunt, disdained to reply and carried on with her speech. This incident was cause for a tightening of sphincters, microphone protocol and members' etiquette—although not enough of the latter to prevent two later references, by members who were standing in their place, to Japs and niggers in the woodpile. The first was uttered by a WW II veteran and former Esquimalt beat cop who, after a brief (1951-'53) stint as a CCF MLA, returned to the legislature for the NDP in 1979. The second came from the lips of a venerable (and venerated) Socred MLA and Minister of Transportation, who was shunted aside by Premier Vander Zalm, with the promise (fulfilled) of having a bridge named after him. Neither man could be accused of conscious racism. They were using expressions they had never associated with cause for offence—the sort that made a younger generation of MLAs on both sides of the aisle wince and have a quiet "afterword" with their elders.

My grandmother, a woman of impressive progressive credentials (for her time) and widow of the Liberal MP (1904-'08) for Yale-Cariboo, insisted on calling Brazil nuts nigger toes, much to the annoyance of my mother, a CCF supporter—notwithstanding her mother's party affiliation, which has never been a reliable measure of progressive thinking. Liberal Senator John Wallace de Beque Farris, founder of Vancouver's most prestigious law firm and member of the closest thing Canada has had to an aristocracy, reacted to criticism of Prime Minister Louis St-Laurent from newly elected Progressive-Conservative and first Chinese-Canadian MP Douglas Jung by calling him "this Chinaman."

Finally, here's one from the last years of the first, Premier W.A.C. Bennett phase of Social Credit government: Agnes Kripps's BOLT speech. It's a striking example of an elected member fearlessly speaking her mind, revealing her heartfelt inner moral core as she advocated for something she believed was in the highest interest of the whole community. She was a Socred MLA for only three years, 1969-'72, but she left a unique and indelible mark on B.C. politics. BOLT has been celebrated in story, song and cyberspace; but there is some dispute among latter-day celebrants over what exactly her acronym stood for: biology of life today; biology of living today; biology of living for today. It was the hippie era, but this last one looks unlike Agnes, or like a joke at her expense, of which there have been many.

A tireless proponent for a ministry of youth, Agnes also believed that sex education was needed; and that in order to achieve "frankness and freedom from inhibition" while avoiding *double entendres* and other smut (a doomed quest), BOLT should replace the word "sex" in all school textbooks and other curriculum materials—and in any other discussion of sex education. As she unveiled her replacement for the "hated word" (note "hated" not "hateful") the House gave vent to yelps of delight and derision—this was too good to be true. "No bolts without nuts." "Why bolt when you can screw?" "You have me bolt upright in my chair." Alberni MLA Howie McDiarmid said he heard opposition leader Bob Strachan say: "I'm going to B-O-L-T off out of here." Finally, there was Agnes's plea to the Speaker: "Won't you please bang that thing of yours." Agnes was beyond help from that or any other quarter. But she sailed on serenely, undaunted and undeterred, through the hail of ridicule.

Interestingly, the jeers came less from the opposition benches than from the new breed of Young Turks on the government side of the aisle. "Bolt upright" was part of a response to Agnes's speech (not an interjection) from Herb Capozzi, Socred back-bencher, stock promoter, former pro football player and son of Pasquale Capozzi, founder of Calona Wines and confidant of the Premier, who was not amused by locker-room humour. The laid-back dudes in loafers from Howe Street—sobriquet for Vancouver's financial zone, which used to house penny-ante bucket-shops that peddled dubious mining shares—were the Social Credit future, taking over from the conventionally upright congregation in lace-ups from up-country. BOLT heralded the end of the "Wacky" Bennett era. After a one-term NDP interlude, the Socreds came roaring back in 1975 under his son Bill, more comfortable in the corporate boardroom than in the stock room of his father's Kelowna hardware store.

— CHAPTER 3(a) —

The Age of Consent and the Age of Majority—
Foundations

The much-vaunted rule of law, and obedience to actual, "positive" laws, are both based on some kind of contract. It's a Burkean one of loyalty to a chain not of servitude but of obligation to past, present and future generations of a community; or it's an exchange of value, whether that's (a) money for commodities or real estate or (b) security of life and property in return for less freedom to do whatever one feels like doing. The first contract could be said to be about the sustaining "spirit of the laws" and the second is obviously more down to earth. In both cases it's often referred to as the social contract at work, and it usually depends on some prior, and surviving, set of (often unwritten) rules and their enforcement (which may have been by threat of ostracism or banishment). Underneath it all is some degree of mutual trust in promises made, a lengthy experience of promises mostly not broken and trust mostly not betrayed. Invasion and colonization throw everything into disarray and dispute or, more often, suppression and oppression.

The history of relations between aboriginal peoples and their unwanted European guests is rife with promises made, withdrawn, broken and denied—and some treaties whose ramifications the parties to them didn't understand, or didn't care about (because of deceitful intentions). Promise-keeping can be jeopardized by inequality within and between parties. The early history of contact between North American aboriginals and Europeans shows evidence of a few exceptional promises kept by the latter—not promising exceptions, unfortunately—until they were no longer at some significant material disadvantage in a strange place. Agreements and treaties may be envisioned, even signed, before trust has been firmly established. But, to make one question out of two old sayings, are they worth whatever they're written on if one of the signatories "speaks with forked tongue"? Northerly North American Indians freely agreed to the terms of trade involved in their exchange of abundant furs for exotic foreign "trinkets." As European demand for furs in shorter, more difficult supply increased, an agreed fair exchange for them became guns and liquor. For a variety of differing reasons both sides came to regret that bargain; but it was unforced, if in hindsight unwise. At the time, European contract law and theory were prepared, with or without documentary proof, to construct a contract from conduct—especially if it could be done to the advantage of the European party in negotiations with non-Europeans. It became increasingly clear to both sides that they were divided, internally as well as from each other, by their assumption of incompatible future considerations; and rancour replaced agreement.

Before there was any idea of a social contract, there was a rudimentary belief among the "rude" people that "a man's house is his castle"—a hovel may not have a moat and a drawbridge, but he had the right to use what little might he had to defend his home and its contents (animal, vegetable or mineral), however humble. Sheer might usually prevailed, on a presumption of feudal ownership rights; but there remained the barely submerged community memory of a wrong having been committed. This sentiment did not travel well, especially to *terra nova, incognita et deserta*—which is what the vast expanses of North America were in the minds of European settlers. Many of them came from England, where revolting peasants would now and then rise up, chanting: "When Adam delved and Eve span/Who was then the gentleman?" The English gentry had already "landed" well in the new land, but there were "lots" more out west for the rabble. As described in Nancy Isenberg's *White Trash*, the flock of retainers accompanying Lords Baltimore and Delaware and others of that ilk got the least arable of the lands their land (and political) lords were given—clay (and its worms) was at times all they had to eat, causing mental and physical damage for generations of the poorest whites. The more adventurous among them never conceived of native Indians having a right to resist B and E on their ancestral homelands. They were just more, but fortunately less abundant, animals. One of my supervisors at LSE was K.C.B. Smellie, author of works on comparative government—if you think his name is funny, how about an LSE philosophy instructor named N.O. Wisdom? Our chats about my MSc (Econ) subject, John Ruskin's writings on political economy, often wandered far off topic to such things as the Chinese approach to Western thought. Mao was very much alive, and K.C.B. opined that when China took over the world, we would all be put in cages as interesting zoological specimens.

Might has a bad conscience that can only be assuaged by convincing itself it's right. Those who deplore that sentiment are mostly not fighting for what they see to be their rights. Trump has a talent for persuading descendants of white settlers that they are the new natives defending their homes against an unholy alliance of quisling liberals and "revolting peasants" from "shithole countries."

Thomas Hobbes and John Locke both waxed a bit "spiritual" in their respective versions of the social contract. Hobbes's "covenant" is more than a contract for "the mutual transferring of right"; it's fundamentally about enduring future performance. The covenanters' authorship of a political sovereign submits each of them to one sovereign will "by plurality of voices," which agreement is "a real unity of them all" (*Leviathan*, ch. 25). A "plurality of voices" may or may not mean a majority of votes; either way, a lot of people may be disaffected (but very "effected") covenanters. The trick (as it were) is to balance fear of others, a natural "passion," with the rational pursuit of felicity in societal life among others—a vain pursuit if one's felicity is not recognized, admired and (both pleasant and potentially painful) envied by others. Hobbes excludes "common peoples' minds" from the covenant's ratiocination because "unless they be tainted with dependence on the potent, or scribbled over with the opinions of their doctors [what a feast those two phrases are for both elite talk of "deplorables" and distrust of professional opinion], they are like clean paper, fit to receive whatsoever by public authority shall be imprinted in them" (*Leviathan*, ch. 30). He considered popular assemblies a "paradise" for orators and for "tyranny" of a more potent speech over a better argument; that allowing all and sundry to deliberate important and difficult matters is "an uncertain trial of a little vainglory" that creates enmities; and that "to be absent from a trial of wits, although those trials are pleasant to the eloquent, is not therefore a grievance to them, unless we will say that it is a grievance to valiant men to be restrained from fighting, because they delight in it" (*On the Citizen*, X, ix).

Locke's version of the social contract sounds more populist. If "the government be dissolved…the majority [not plurality]… may employ all that power in making laws for the community…and executing those laws by officers of their own appointing; and then the form of the government is a perfect democracy." "Perfect democracy" occurs when a government dissolves, and law-making and enforcement pass to the majority "having the whole power of the community naturally in them"

(*Second Treatise*, section 158). In parliamentary democracies, sovereignty belongs to the executive branch when the legislature has dissolved for an election. Locke indirectly endorses legislative inactivity, by saying that "frequent meetings of the legislative and long continuations of their assemblies, without necessary occasion, could not but be burdensome to the people, and must necessarily in time produce more dangerous inconveniences" (section 156).

State-supported social contracts may be effective, but only insofar as they rely on a supportive consensus more than law enforcement. The ways in which a "contract" is enforced in the criminal underworld (in life as well as in lore) are not confined to that world. A lot of money in global circulation has been laundered but still "grey," unbleached of its origins and continuing criminal connections. Governments using 3Ps (public-private partnerships) to fund their projects often discover, too late, that they are being used by silent partners to both legitimize ill-gotten gains and make more of them. The social costs—underpaid, unprotected labour; incomplete, unsafe buildings; political corruption and public distrust—are adulteration and counterfeit of a jurisdiction's wealth. A Canadian case in point is Quebec's construction industry, whose "mafia" connections have been subject to a long series of judicial inquiries. Another window has been opened on the public fisc becoming enmeshed in global "high" finance (and the low-lifes among its leading lights) by its efforts to find, follow and spend the money, now fungible to an unprecedented degree: Montreal-based engineering firm SNC-Lavalin bribing a Libyan dictator and being protected from prosecution by the Canadian government. A plausible (if strangely fruitful) line of inquiry might be any "grey" money trail to the gulags of North Korea, a client state of China, through which investors could (in contravention of their countries' laws and international sanctions) partner in the manufacture of goods outsourced to the cheapest labour of all. Mangling a familiar quotation, give a capitalist a long line of credit, however discreditable, and he'll make a noose for his own neck.

One cause of the social contract's loss of political traction has been the detachment of economic science from the study of political economy and economic history, accompanied by the displacement in political thought and action of all other public goods by economic growth—"It's the economy, stupid." It is indeed, an engine of productivity whose operation depends on some of the wealth it generates being spent on a social infrastructure subsidy; this engine wants all sorts of services, from public education to public highways, but not as a capital cost on its balance sheet.

About 85 years after Adam Smith's *Wealth of Nations* laid the foundation for economics as the separate study of an autonomous sphere of societal activity, John Ruskin took on the "death" science in the shape of one its least value-free practitioners, John Stuart Mill. The Mill-Ruskin engagement was a case of ships that pass in the night. Neither side came to grips with the other, in spite of both authors having been educated in the "Greats" (or classical writings) tradition—so too was Smith, whose *oeuvre* could have helped bridge the gap for them. In "Ad Valorem," chapter 4 of *Unto This Last*, Ruskin says that wealth is "possession of the valuable by the valiant," and that valor means strength in life and for life; hence to be valuable is "to avail towards life." He is famous for saying elsewhere that the so-called captains of industry should take their title seriously: a sense of honour and duty to others is the essence of leadership in all walks of life. What bearing, an economist may ask, does any of that have on market forces, prices and wages, production, distribution and consumption? Starting with the last one—consumption, not the last toiler, who should be paid as much as the first in line—Ruskin says that "all *essential* production is for the mouth…and the wealth of a nation is only to be estimated by what it consumes" (not just how much). Then his final thrust: "The want of any clear sight of this fact [the economic importance of consumption] is the capital error, issuing in rich interest and revenue of error among the political economists. Their minds are continually set on money-gain, not mouth-gain...." (*Unto This Last: Four Essays on the Principles of Political Economy* (1862), Crofts Classics, 1967, p. 85).

The poetry of his polemic aside, Ruskin had some insight into a major defect of global finance capitalism: too much seed, not enough sustenance; money-making is not wealth production. In spite of all their efforts—in particular, quantitative easing—those in charge of the money supply have had little success shifting the wealth out of hedge funds, corporate bonds and trusts, and into productive circulation. Can we infer from the ease with which stock markets recovered from their first, pandemic-induced, panicky loss of several thousand points that they represented no more than numbers on jobbers' computer screens, and not real wealth? Ruskin is also a source for the revival of an old line of attack on and possible penetration of political belief systems closed to normative discourse and value-driven argument.

• • • • •

Hobbes was a logical and linguistic nominalist. In other words, all our words are only about words, and "truth consisteth in the right ordering of names in our affirmations"—names for our thoughts about what we experience and declare "one to another for mutual utility and conversation" (*Leviathan*, ch. 4). Hobbes was a forerunner of Benthamite utilitarians. Could he have inspired Karl Kraus to say, in *The Last Days of Mankind*, that "a breakdown in values begins with a breakdown of meaning in language"? Not unless Hobbes is read as a satirist. Like Plato, he distrusted literary art in general: "playing with our words," the building blocks of a shared reality, is suspect because of its potential for deception. So much for satire and irony. However, he was not averse to deploying metaphor, as in his witticism about how "it is with the mysteries of our religion, as with wholesome pills for the sick, which swallowed whole, have the virtue to cure; but chewed, are for the most part cast up again without effect" (*Leviathan*, ch. 32).

The following is an example of how a single word can be divisive—at the same time helping to explicate, but not resolve, any misunderstanding. To assume something means taking it for granted, as understood in the same way by all concerned; it also means accepting and undertaking some responsibility or obligation. In old English common law, "assumpsit" meant the latter. When Europeans and Indians partied and parleyed, with exchange of gifts and hearty consumption of food and liquid refreshments, the Europeans understood, assumed that they were going to get Indian land in return for hosting the celebrations; the Indians thought they were all celebrating the Europeans agreeing to recognize Indian title to that land. They were both "sitting in a sump," a swamp of misunderstanding and mischief (etymologically minus head; the chiefs were not thinking clearly—because they had consumed too much foreign firewater?). There was no underlying agreement or consensus, no meeting of minds. Culture and language aside, the biggest problem was European land hunger (and dreams of hidden gold and other treasure). Cruelly honest whites foresaw that the pressure of their ever-increasing numbers could lead to the total dispossession and even extermination of the land's aboriginal inhabitants.

Is the following wordplay about words that may be used to "put lipstick on a pig" itself a form of deception? Words beginning with "ass" make up a special group in any English dictionary. Chief among them is "assassin," leader of the pack for its sheer ass power. Its double-cheek ass is indispensable for a functioning ass hole. The rest, in descending order of thrust, are all half-assed. "Assail" and "assault" are weakened by their non-physical meanings, often accompanied by expressions of mock horror and outrage. The middle of the pack—"assess(ment)," "assign(ation)," "assume" and so on, even in the case of "assert(ion)"—contain seeds of uncertainty, procrastination and prevarication. The third layer is an "assembly" of sugary deceit promising the comforts of harmony and unity: "assent," "assistance," "association," "assuage" and "assure"—assimilation is felt to be a good thing by many immigrants, less so by aboriginals. More on the ass ent of con sent, shortly.

— CHAPTER 3(b) —

Nobody mistakes a majority for unanimity, but electoral minorities can be treated as irrelevant or mistaken, and in either case expected to closet their opposition, accept majority rule and agree to "make it unanimous." In places where large majorities are forced fabrications, active and noisy minorities tend to (be) disappear(ed). Consent is often understood to require individual willingness, although that does not mean it is either well-informed or enthusiastic. Absence of overt dissent can be a result of either pervasive (often official) intimidation or of suspended judgment on a complex issue. Consensus and consent are sometimes confused—understandably, because they're at etymological root the same. Nor is consensus the same thing as unanimity, as in everybody thinking as one; it may have been induced (or seduced) to produce an appearance of unanimity in thought as well as action. Where free expression in debate is the rule, consensus or a meeting of minds is usually arrived at after a lengthy exchange of views in which opposition has been softened or abandoned—because of a (common) sense about where the argument is heading and a desire to not prolong it by flogging an exhausted and trailing horse ("going along to get along" and get to a decision). A vestigial problem (one that may later rupture, like an appendix) is the assumed compliance of pliable dissenters being later seen, by both an entrenched majority and resurgent minorities, as a form of complicity.

Consent is generally felt to be crucial in any relationship, commercial and personal as well as political—and in parental nurturing of children, even at an early age. It is also felt that it should be informed consent, although the degree of being informed to qualify as consent may differ according to the relationship. And it should be free of coercion, intimidation or misapprehension. Then comes the reality of consent. How can one have consented to all the terms and conditions of a contract if pages and pages of it in small print are written in a way designed to bewilder anyone with no legal training? Why are people otherwise deemed minors treated as adults ready to consent to assuming the responsibility of parenthood simply because they are post-pubescent? Which laws and bylaws require citizens' express consent and for which can it be taken for granted? Most people seem to agree that (1) some contractual conditions are so crucial to fairness that they can be assumed as given; (2) age is an adequate guide to degree of fitness for different kinds of responsibility; and (3) no society can function if every act or regulation must have the express consent of a majority, let alone everybody.

Consent as the firm expression of a free and independent will may be assumed—even if in some cases it is unknowing and in others grudging—by way of the notion of assent. In constitutional monarchies the Crown as head of state says nothing, expresses no intention and certainly no opinion, when assenting to legislative bills enacted by an elected legislature. It seems like a royal favour being granted, one that could be withdrawn as quickly and silently as it was given. Assent is valid only if given without exception. Silence will be heard as consent; if you seriously dissent, you better speak up—unless your "constitution" (including in a personal sense) is apolitical. (See Alan Bennett, *The Uncommon Reader*,

p. 56, for "…the Queen nodding assent though not always agreement.")
A long tradition of silent assent to legislative acts makes a constitutional
monarch publicly voicing dissent so irrelevant as to be a legal nullity.
(See the TV movie *Charles III*). The U.K.'s ten-year-old Supreme Court
decided unanimously, on 14 September 2019, that (if only to spare the
monarch) she had been deceived by PM Boris Johnson when she was
asked to assent to a parliamentary prorogation. Her customary assent
to such a request was in this instance void and of no effect because his
advice to her "was unlawful, void and of no effect…and the order-in-
council to which it led…should be quashed." Shortly thereafter, he won
a big general election victory, and a few months later recovered from a
serious bout with Covid-19. Score 2-1 for parliamentary democracy?

Democratic systems of long standing—ones whose rules and conventions have evolved and been accepted over many generations—have established that consent to what a majority of the people's representatives
decide is in the public interest can be assumed (until electorally and/or
legally appealed). Constitutional monarchies' royal assent presupposes
transfer of a people's sovereignty to the legislatures and governments
that elections create. Transfer to the former is partially revoked by continuity in the exercise of executive power by the latter—i.e., PMs or
Premiers who have the confidence of an elected legislature—in the
name of the Crown.

Continuous operation of any political system depends on a lot of un-
spoken and unreserved assent. In John Henry (Cardinal) Newman's
Grammar of Assent, it's a silent, internal movement of the will—towards
what is less important than its being away from disobedience. Does democracy depend on something suspiciously like one of the faith "mysteries" of religious belief? If so, this suffers by comparison with the idea
of a founding social contract; but it too can be vague and a bit of a mystery. The "pills" (Hobbes) of political doctrine are mysteries more likely

to be "swallowed whole," thereby curing civil disaffection and disturbance. If "chewed," they may give rise to those political maladies and worse—as with what "chewing" the Bible, in many vulgar tongues, did for Europe's medieval religious *pax*.

• • • • •

The "mystery" of government and its acceptance by the governed is encountering infidel mysteries propagated by opponents, if not enemies, of liberal democracy, which they brand a mismatch (the illegitimate offspring) of liberalism and populism. It's so much easier to fight it with other mysteries—and conspiracy theories—than with evidence and analysis that invite lengthy argument and counter-argument. An educational introduction to citizenship in a mixed system of government is what used to be called civics. If it is thought of as Sunday-school learning by rote, that demeans it by infecting it with religiosity and/or the notion of a civil religion. In his inaugural address as Professor of Government at the London School of Economics, Michael Oakeshott lamented the disfavour into which political education (the idea and the term) had fallen, tainted by totalitarian regimes' propaganda broadcasts and their "endless repetition of what was scarcely worth saying once."

The controversial demand that political education be legislated into all school and college curricula gained new pertinence after it was discovered that social media ads designed to foment racist and other divisive fears among American voters (and viewed by millions of them) during the 2016 election campaign were Russian-state-backed. The murkily complex global network of money laundromats makes the funding trail for these deliberately misleading messages hard to find and follow. Preventing more such "invasion" is made more difficult by a Supreme Court decision that money is speech protected by the First

Amendment. Also, the long history of "Voice of America" and other "liberty radio" broadcasts to "enslaved" nations has made them disinclined to see any difference between the broadcasts of Russian (and other, home-grown) "troll factories" and the sort of thing U.S. political parties do to each other, with ever-increasing verbal violence, in their campaign advertising.

The underlying problem is more one of domestic political illiteracy than of foreign interference. The first line of defence against foreign interventions is not cyber-warfare but making people more aware, from an early age, of how their government and politics work—and how sometimes they do not. If citizens were better equipped to put news (in the press or on the Web), infomercials and PSAs into a wider context, of their own and other countries' history and politics, they would be less easily alarmed or fooled by denial and distortion of facts. The kind of fearful ignorance that makes people susceptible to improbable rumours and conspiracy theories is validated by a President who seems compelled to spread them—and said "I love the non-college-educated" who voted for him in a 2016 presidential primary. Trump used his rallies, a pre-presidential bully pulpit, to help divide American society into two warring totalitarian opinion regimes ("tribal epistemologies"). Q-Anon, a mysterious social media blog that appears to be a source of news for Trump, energetically spreads stories about Democratic child abuse and ritual murder; and has now taken control of some Republican primaries. A Q-Anon believer was elected to the House of Representatives, whose Covid mask-wearing rules she rejects, saying (as if she were an abortion rights activist): "My body, my choice."

— CHAPTER 4(a) —

Different Worlds?

There is a quasi-contractual relationship between aboriginal and non-aboriginal Canadians whose depth can be measured in layers of history. As for geography, Canadians continue to be overawed by theirs; Americans have overwhelmed theirs. Canada's climatic misfortune, compared to the mostly temperate zones of the United States and their agricultural bounty, had the beneficial side-effect of discouraging huge waves of immigrant-refugees, thus limiting occasions for conflict with native populations. First "contact" (a bland word for invasion) with Europeans soon grew into promiscuous violence and their looting of ancient civilizations and cultures. The so-called Columbian Exchange ushered in the Anthropocene age or epoch of human activity and global commerce, by bringing the American continents out of their oceanic isolation and into an already existing system of primarily land-based trade in goods and people. Using a geological-sounding term to describe this new age is fitting because it began with the asteroid-like arrival on Amerindian shores of ships full of life forms (animal, vegetable and microbial) that might as well have come from outer space. Northern tribes and confederacies tended to combine with as much as against British and French invaders contending for the "new" land;

but they too succumbed to disease and other European imports, as well as to superior numbers and firepower. Aboriginals in the U.S. and Canada have been marginalized on and off reserve, but have made some demographic recovery. In Canada, an additional Métis population has grown out of intermarriage or cohabitation with early French and Scottish traders. Relations were long much more mercantile than in the U.S., whose more hospitable topography meant that settlement expanded faster and intruded more forcibly on native lives, and "spreads" (farms, ranches and towns) became more important than trading-posts.

The Canadian nation was built in part on what could be called aboriginal fallout from the American Revolution. From the 18th century to the 20th, from the Atlantic seaboard to the Pacific, from Mohawk Valley to Chesterman's Beach, lands used communally (if not always peacefully) by aboriginals were pre-empted by settlers and by speculators who pretended to be acting as agents of the Crown. A major Indian mistake was a persistent belief that the "great white father [or mother]" had the power as well as the duty to protect native land usage customs as natural rights. Alan Taylor argues convincingly that Indians lived by a creed that gift-giving was both act and symbol of friendship. Meetings with Europeans to discuss matters of common concern, to pow-wow with lengthy circumlocution, to exchange gifts (with a promise of their money to follow), created binding ties of mutual moral obligation— and not an Indian promise to cede their lands to others. Governor Simcoe of Upper Canada was one of those British officials who played nice, and for time, with Six Nations "savages" in the struggle to repel American settler and military incursions. His American counterpart, Governor Clinton of New York, became a model for the new republic's aboriginal relations policy: aggressive double-dealing. Simcoe denounced a "Right of preemption, or Speculation, words justifying great Swindling Transactions of selling the Indians' Lands to pay off the Debts of the United States."

"The chiefs understood that speculators who bought a 'preemption right' would, to recoup their investment, relentlessly pressure the Indians to forsake possession. Only as federally recognized 'freemen' and 'sole proprietors of the soil' could the Iroquois fend off the insidious threat of preemption, which entailed a future property in Indian dispossession." (Taylor, *The Divided Ground: Indians, Settlers and the Northern Borderlands of the American Revolution*, 2006, pp. 269-72).

Once U.S. federal power was established, American leaders, from Washington on down the line and down the years, have used their bully pulpit to instill a doctrine of white (mostly Anglo-Saxon) cultural superiority to, among others, native Indians. (President Andrew Jackson made it clear that he thought U.S. policy should be continued enslavement of negroes and extermination of aboriginals. On the other hand, Gen. Robert E. Lee, when surrendering to Ulysses S. Grant, was mightily relieved that a swarthy member of Grant's staff whose hand he was expected to shake turned out to be not a black man but, he joked, "a real American."). One Oneida chief conceded Indian "weakness" for liquor, writing that "if we Indians must bear this reproach of loving Rum, the White Man certainly loves money" (*Divided Ground*, p. 388). Genetic alcoholism can be a non-aboriginal problem as well. Second, and not unrelated to that, we are all, aboriginal and non-aboriginal alike, enmeshed in a global system of exchange whose medium is money, from Thai baht to bit-coins, from IOUs to credit default swaps. Its convenience is such that we can't seem to live without it; but we can't honestly think it's inherently, unquestionably, unreservedly superior to pre-capitalist, pre-industrial ways of life.

The same sorts of things can be said about "aboriginal affairs" in the Canadian nation-state, where all land is held by the Crown for prospective development by public and/or private money; and all subject to being mine(d)—in both senses of the word "mine." As Obama (famously or infamously, depending on one's partisanship) said: "You didn't build [that business] yourself." Self-help claims should always be qualified by some self-denying recognition of what others—many others not just of your family and associates but of a whole community's previous generations—did to lay the indispensable foundations for "your" success. All capital is societal capital. As a sidebar on that, any tax on short-term financial speculation should (and could without danger to stock market trading in general) be many percentage points higher than James Tobin's modest proposal almost 50 years ago. After all, capital gains are a form of rent drawn from economic activity as well being one of its stimuli; and shareholders are rentiers (a French word with unfortunate parasitical connotations).

— CHAPTER 4(b) —

Vancouver Island's Douglas Treaties of 1850-'54 promised aboriginals hunting and fishing rights in perpetuity over territories they had "sold" to Governor Sir James Douglas. If you stray off the main trails behind Island View Beach (on the east side of Saanich Peninsula) and into Tsawout territory, you may encounter young men with rifles—for hunting game, one would like to think—being carried in a brandishing sort of way. This, and signs, tell you that you are on aboriginal land (by treaty) rather than recreational space (CRD Parks); and on a site for scientific study of invasive species (of the plant sort only—so far—according to those who set it up). Debate continues about the status of these treaty rights, including Douglas's standing and authority to sign for them on behalf of the Crown. A triumvirate of Douglas, Hudson's Bay Company chief factor Peter Ogden and Dr. John McLoughlin helped negotiate ceding HBC territory to future U.S. states Oregon and Washington and looping the 49ᵗʰ parallel in a way that kept all of Vancouver Island in what was to become Canada. It's of some interest that they have descendants among at least one of the south Island Indian tribes. Of different (and probably less) interest is the new border's failure to take into account Point Roberts, which became a U.S. exclave, the part-time home of mostly Canadian vacationers and dependent for its water on the neighbouring B.C. municipality.

In northeastern B.C. some aboriginal land is covered by one of the old numbered treaties, trans-provincial Treaty 8. In 2000, the Nisga'as got legal title to a big chunk of their traditional lands in northwestern B.C. through the long-sought Nisga'a Treaty. It was thought by many to be the template for a multi-party process of negotiating modern treaties elsewhere. A basis for disagreeing is that its enactment left unresolved an overlapping claim from the Gitxsan-Wet'suwet'ens, who began the long-lasting "landmark" Delgamuukw v. British Columbia lawsuit. Inferring from oral history of a group memory that there had been an exchange of promises, a kind of contractual obligation, the Supreme Court of Canada went on to rule that certain aboriginal rights had been legally established. It leap-frogged over political decision-making, and governments were left lagging behind and in constitutional arrears.

It is a cliché that the federal Indian Act treats aboriginals as wards of the state—like all clichés, it became one because of its portion of truth. It's the paternalist zombie at the table where the tripartite process to honour a putative and imprecise contract with First Nations drags on. Funding authorized by the Indian Act sustains and prolongs the treaty process. The act is seen by both natives and non-natives as a colonial relic and impediment to progress towards a more equal relationship. Aboriginals have long been treated as interchangeably children and adults—which helps explain their militancy. Such treatment is inconsistent with the language, however un-legal or politically slippery, of both old contracts and new treaties. A "contract" with children, offering them something that will induce them to do their homework, is not a contract but a bribe. If they're invited to negotiate its terms, parental and/or teacher authority is reduced to intermittent *in loco parentis*. The hope of some aboriginals that a distant magisterial (magical?) parent would protect them—a belief happily encouraged by some non-aboriginal officials—was a delusion dispelled for most of them long ago.

Non-aboriginal governments at every level have been pursuing the phantom of political peace, convinced it can be caught and kept through so-called modern treaties. A recent obstacle placed in the path of that quest is the Supreme Court of Canada's Chilcotin decision that "unceded" land—territory in what is generally known as Canada not either covered by treaty or conquered (whatever that means)—may be considered subject to aboriginal claims based on traditional usages. A right of public access over (or through, by legally disputed rights-of-way) un-subdivided private land has often been asserted. There is now the prospect of Crown lands and private properties that have been bought and sold on a fee-simple basis being subject to various reclaimed, as yet undetermined but justiciable, aboriginal uses. Both arbitration panels and law courts will become involved in attempts to resolve conflicts between aboriginal and non-aboriginal usage rights. What about conflicting aboriginal assertions of right, as in a dam project that would result in submersion of fur-trapping land? Discuss. This exam has no time limit.

Time has also radically transformed the real-world conditions in which we all live. Those who believe that a political settlement can only be achieved by modern treaties, through which aboriginal peoples regain (some of) their former autonomy, have to face an uncomfortable fact. On or off reserve, most aboriginals live in the same material world as most non-aboriginals: the world of Costco, Dollarama, fast food and countless gas-guzzling journeys. Its Canadian vortex is Alberta's Fort McMurray (the town that couldn't say no to becoming the world's biggest monster truck rally), whose satanic pits shudder at the thought of processing plants consuming more fuel than they generate, destroying the water of life to make the oil of industry, and, worst of all for finance capital, being made uneconomic by the geopolitics of a global oil market. As the surrounding boreal forest becomes hotter and drier earlier and earlier, tar-sands oil extraction and production operations (and delivery of the product by pipeline) are threatened by the climate change they help cause. The year-over-year increase in northern wildfires' size and speed is a warning sign for not only Fort Mac.

Aboriginals face a Hobson's choice: live more like their pre-contact ancestors and be pushed into a vanishing corner; or participate in self-alienating exploitation of their lands and waters—alienating because finance capital works by putting a price tag on everything. Quebec is neither a major nor a minor player in the global capitalist economy, but is protected by Canadian federal power from the full effects of wholesale "dumping" and other hostile kinds of competition. France struggles to hold onto its identity while part of an international system of trade and finance that puts constant pressure on every nation's cherished traditions and institutions as well as on its major corporations. The aboriginal field of dreams, that vast Canadian space available for aboriginal enterprise, is being fought over by clashing armies of natural resource prospectors and preservationists, who all say they have the best interests of indigenous peoples at heart.

In places where final settlement has been achieved, some native governments have chosen to engage in the hospitality and recreation industries, to contract out or themselves operate campgrounds and eco-cultural tours, as well as hotels and casinos, on their traditional territory. The Tsawouts are an interesting variation. First, they declined to participate in the B.C. treaty process. Then, in 2006, they entered into a First Nations GST agreement with the feds, whereby they can use tax revenue collected on their reserve land to purchase additional land and/or seed economic development. Tsawout councils seem to have approved full-on commercial engagement with their neighbours and a larger world, as evidenced by the Pat Bay Highway's "billboard alley" that runs through their land. It would also seem that not all members of the band are in complete agreement with policies that open Tsawout lands to non-native commerce. Recall the young Tsawout men with rifles at Island View Beach. The one I spoke to seemed torn between confronting non-natives who traipsed over his land and joining two other Tsawouts who had built a stand from which they were selling the trespassers hot dogs and soft drinks.

— CHAPTER 5 —

Representing Aboriginals

"Native society is not static. The things the native people have said… should not be regarded as a lament for a lost way of life, but as a plea for an opportunity to shape their own future, out of their own past. They are not seeking to entrench the past, but to build on it." So said Chief Elijah Smith, president of the Yukon Native Brotherhood, almost 50 years ago. More recently, Jose Kusugak, president of the Inuit Tapiriit Kanatami, said that because of climate change, "we face the possibility of having to completely reinvent what it means to be Inuit." These words point to the closing of a gap between Western science and traditional ecological knowledge; and to a path of collaboration that could be both renovation and restoration.

Change has been much more wounding for aboriginals than for non-aboriginals; it has been deeply traumatic. But both have been more objects than subjects of contemporary cultural acceleration. Western majoritarian democracies think, or pretend, they can control what is still nervously called the "progress" of the human race; but it feels like a tide carrying all boats who knows where, and the only respite is finding some back eddy. We are torn by incompatible world-views. Some who advocate a U-turn to ancestral ways of life (or imagined ones) react violently against the force majeure of modernity. So what has an animist minority living more or less quietly among a secularist majority got to do with violent conflicts between murderous monotheists, or between them and infidels? We have been lucky with our most demanding issue, as politicians of all stripes have been calling it for decades: relations between non-aboriginal and aboriginal Canadians. People impatient with those who cannot accept the Western modernity package even as they live in, with and from it should ponder Joseph Conrad's words in *Under Western Eyes*: "It is not for us, the staid lovers calmed by the possession of a conquered liberty, to condemn without appeal the fierceness of thwarted desire." He was not talking about a desire to share in the spoils of (hoped-for) victory over poverty and ignorance. He was no Frantz Fanon fiercely identifying with the "wretched of the earth"; but he bore witness to "the horror, the horror" casually inflicted on them by Westerners. An outsider himself, he had the integrated alien's ability to see things from an impartial perspective—which, of course, no party to any serious dispute wants to hear, especially if it's one that has been "settled" in favour of one party for many years if not decades, even centuries.

In the notable case of the conflict between Israelis and Palestinians, modernizing Zionists and other Jews were alien invaders who considered themselves culturally superior and the religiously rightful owners of the disputed land. (They also tried to convince themselves they would share "their new" land with its Arab inhabitants.) Such variably self-righteous motives re-enacted what drove dispossession of the aboriginal inhabitants of the American, Australian and African continents—except that the Africans outnumbered and outlasted their unwanted European "guests" (will it be the same with their new Chinese "benefactors"?).

· · · · ·

Some of this book's chapters 14-16 talk about the power of deluded thinking and malign (or simply careless) words of disrespect to unleash inter-communal violence. Taken literally, Hobbes's "war of every man against every man" is a comically inflated version of a drunken brawl. A more trenchant version of Hobbes's aphorism is T.S. Eliot's dramatic words, when he was asked to make a political forecast: "people shooting each other in the streets"—now being borne out in cinemas, shopping malls, schools, churches and other meeting-places. And a lot of it has no direct or clear connection with Islamist threats of mass murder. There is evidence in support of the thesis that fanatical religious, racist or nationalist fundamentalism is a public face or "cover" for motivation rooted in criminal gang psychology. Describing his Irish childhood, Colm Tóibín says everyone knew, from schoolyard behaviour, which kids would grow up to be IRA gunmen.

Hard-core racists, no matter how soothing their public utterances, want civil war and an end to politics, an opening for them to dictate and enforce their permanently divisive solution. The sort of genocidal rage that fuelled and was fuelled by Hitler is off the scale, which makes it too easy for use as an argument against racism. Saying "Never again" to racial extermination does not work as a practical defence against racial exclusion and subjugation. Racial mixing, treating members of any group as individuals first and foremost, is seen by more than a few people as not a remedy but as a danger to allegedly more stable homogenous societies. And policies that prize individual fulfillment above all other good things face a strong minority-group feeling of safety in numbers of familiar faces. A minority's strong sense of and dependence on its common good can be both a microcosm of a larger community of interests and values and a prototype for that community working towards greater equality of social worth, regardless of individuals' qualifications, certificates, diplomas, awards, etc.

Some said Bill Wilson was a racist when, as a member of a Union of B.C Indian Chiefs council, he said: "We should've killed you all." But he was simply stating the obvious. The "should" was a Hobbesian one of logical necessity—and it was an obligation that Indians have always lacked the means to act on. It could also be said that Wilson was referring to an invasion of ideas as well as of people, which invites comparison with the time-bomb reaction of Islamic jihadists to the imposition of Western values through the global reach of social media and other communications. "Jihadi Bill" saw that, with or without re-education camps (residential schools), Canadian aboriginals were being stripped of their identity: consciousness of themselves in a world they had lived in for thousands of years. It was the invasion of the soul-snatchers, albeit without conscious snatching intent— unlike ancestral artifacts, which, reluctantly in some cases, are gradually being returned. The land snatch is another thing, and not so easily resolved.

That slippery word "spirituality" has been at hidden play again, in the emergence of Wet'suwet'en hereditary chiefs from the spirit world to blockade the road to a natural gas pipeline project on their traditional "unceded" lands. This project was approved by an elected Wet'suwt'en tribal council. The mystery (for non-aboriginal observers, as always) is the relationship between council and chiefs. To say that the hereditary chiefs speak for the whole traditional territory and not just the "reserve" land does not help. It sounds like some constitutional monarch wanting to revert to the long-disused authority of his divine-right forebears. Who speaks with ultimate authority in negotiations between aboriginal and non-aboriginal governments? The former can say with some justification that they have to deal with two levels of government, federal and provincial. But they are both at the table. What happens when, it would appear, chiefs and councillors are at cross-purposes, and the former discover that the latter have green-lit a pipeline on their (whose?) land? Who's speaking with forked tongue now? Non-aboriginal frustration matches aboriginal outrage, which spread across the country to blockade rail transport of goods for export and for distribution to Canadians, including aboriginal ones. Non-aboriginal protesters in support of the hereditary chiefs are, we can only hope, learning about the political reality behind the chiefs' spiritual connection with the lands, and transportation corridors, they claim sovereignty over; and we hope that the rest of us may get some practical advice on how to resolve this. Tribal matriarchs on the barricades should remember that a few years ago some native women rose up in protest at the inequitable way too many chiefs and their "first families" have shared federal grants, other economic benefits and political power with tribe members at large. Have they found a new voice on elective councils? Who votes for them, who do they represent, and on the basis of what sort of membership? Questions about political legitimacy on reserve and unceded non-reserve lands need to be answered.

•　•　•　•　•

One aboriginal worry is creeping assimilation by economic stealth more than by political compulsion. The continuing advance of such auto-acculturation differs from self-acculturation, which implies a degree of conscious community control over what is happening. It can also be seen as a form of resistance that converts the isolation of reserve life into pride of place. Acculturation is a word that makes both aboriginal and non-aboriginal people think of official, touristic multiculturalism's costumes-and-folk-dancing stereotypes. A political refuge from that fate, aboriginal-only legislative assembly seats, has been tried in some jurisdictions (e.g., New Zealand). Fulfillment of the best-known Canadian form of that aspiration—a fourth level of jurisdiction—would require a new constitution, a dim and distant prospect.

Canadian aboriginals have long-standing treaty rights that cross provincial borders, and some uncertain ones crossing the international border between Canada and the U.S. The Jay Treaty gave native Indians extensive rights of cross-border travel; but the War of 1812 between the U.K. and the U.S. abrogated that treaty. In practice, the two border services make it relatively easy for regular family-visit and employment border-crossing. Two exceptions are, in the west, members of the Washington-state-based Colville tribal group exercising what they say is their right to hunt on lands of the B.C. Arrow Lakes band, deemed legally extinct but part of the same Salishan language group; and, in the east, Akwesasne Mohawks trying to ease restrictions on travel, for the usual family and employment reasons, between parts of reserve lands split by the Canada-U.S. border, which runs through several lakes and rivers. All of this raises intractable issues of national sovereignty and international law.

A more pressing matter is aboriginal participation at senior Canadian government decision-making levels. Their own most widely accepted representative body is the Assembly of First Nations; but there are others who don't always agree with the AFN. Could they all agree on one-person-one-vote election, by all eligible aboriginal persons in Canada, of rep-by-pop(ulation share) aboriginal representatives in the federal parliament? They would be eligible to vote for national-party candidates or independents in their constituency as well. Might there be, in addition, some sort of quota of seats in cabinet, and further, a requirement that those members be either elected or appointed (or some mixture of both) by the AFN and other such bodies? The precedent is agreements, written and unwritten, about Quebec "national" quotas in the Senate, on the Supreme Court and in cabinet. If any such scheme were enacted, it should have a sunset clause enabling a revisit of the experiment after two or three years' experience. Aboriginals are as likely as non-aboriginals to express dissatisfaction with the experiment.

— CHAPTER 6 —

Representation as Re-Presentation

Representative democracy voices voters' opinions in the legislative assembly, where the government has to listen—for how long and how attentively are both up to the government. Any parliamentary government has to keep in mind that it needs a full House of active, engaged members and their connection to the electorate, regardless of party affiliation, if it wants to be seen to be doing the people's business. When the Liberals won every legislative assembly seat in New Brunswick's 1987 provincial election, the first thing the new government did was try to figure out how to give representation in assembly debate to the party that came second in the popular vote. Various schemes were discussed, some were tried, none were satisfactory, and political opposition was left to the press. (Election by proportional representation instead of traditional first-past-the-post could have been a solution, but that was for another place and another time.)

Some of our most electable MLAs have been ones who speak, not in a multitude of tongues but in tongues of the multitude, faithfully retailing a wide range of opinion in their constituencies, unafraid of contradictions and incoherence. They have succeeded—and succeeded in being re-elected—by dint of not trying too hard to toe the party line and show off their knowledge of the party platform jigsaw. They do not feel they must compose, for the edification (and boredom) of their listeners, an intellectually watertight defence of their party's policy positions. They instinctively recognize that such an effort tends to be exclusionary, a costly tendency in politics.

Knowingly or not, they operate on the basis that there is no sustainable unified theory of the world, and no political philosophy able to imagine all eventualities. They subscribe to Isaiah Berlin's pluralistic teaching that strict adherence to a principle is the moral course so long as one is prepared to accept that one may be rationally (hence morally) obliged to alter it because of changed circumstances—"Principles are not less sacred because their duration cannot be guaranteed." He expressed a related idea in a more allegorical way: the difference between human foxes and human hedgehogs. The MLAs referred to here don't huddle in holes; they don't hang around the refuge of home base. Like foxes, they roam around, sniffing out new ideas and fresh prospects; and like magpies, they pick up other people and opinions a bit indiscriminately.

Much-reviled party discipline can help build a windbreak between politicians and the vagaries of public opinion. Party platforms can restrain partisans, compelling them to prioritize and compromise some of their views in order to defend the policy set they have made such efforts to embrace for the electoral sake of their party. That may work for a party's so-called base—or not, as with Donald Trump's angrily anarchic anti-party followers. Is he in control of his crowd, as he seems to be, when he refers to "his" loyal Republicans, whom it (rightly) thinks are his submissive stooges? (The exceptional Senator Romney, who voted for Trump's removal from office, is beyond the pale.) Or does he take cues from his rally crowd, like the one that replied to his weak (and inaccurate) description of Speaker Pelosi's reaction to his State of the

Union address with a favourite chant: "Lock her up"? He looked a bit surprised, but shrugged, as if to say: "I'll go along with that." Did he have any choice?

Candidates competing for election to a legislature may campaign on their ability to be more representative of a constituency's length and breadth of opinion, to be the one who speaks to power for more people, if not all of them. Elected representatives are supposed to speak for all of "you"— which means acting for all of you, by trying to think for you as if they were you. Representation is a form of re-presentation, in which, however hard they may try not to, candidates and elected members translate their constituents' words into their own, and in the process make constituents' goals fit members' own. Political authorization to take over electors' views in this way is a hard act to swallow. Mark Lilla had this to say in an essay on the U.S Tea Party's rise: "Representative democracy is a tricky system; it must first give citizens voice as individuals, and then echo their collective voice back at them in policies they approve of." Their voices are not being ignored but recast as systematic policy. But "more voices has meant less echo for" many and therefore less attention. Ordinary people's voices have been drowned out by panels of partisan pundits, sound-bite artists and candidate surrogates all doing commentary in their own echo chamber. Candidates themselves feel compelled to give Instagram responses to everything flung at them. There are fewer and fewer non-hectoring voices of mediation.

· · · · ·

At one end of the representation theory spectrum is an oft-cited letter from Edmund Burke to influential members of his Bristol constituency. He told those who wrote in protest at his position on a particular issue that, whether or not they understood or liked it, they had elected him to make up his own mind about what he should do, on their behalf, when this or any other matter came up for a vote. In a letter collected in his *Correspondence*, he expresses himself in a more conciliatory tone: "I cannot indeed take it upon me to say that I have the honour to *follow* the sense of the people. The truth is I *met it on my way*, while I was pursuing their interest according to my own ideas." He was not, he said, elected to poll his constituents whenever he had a difficult choice to make. Political scientists and pollsters have discovered voting behaviour so uninformed it resembles Pin the Tail on the Donkey. But election is choice, and doubly so: representatives are elected to make operational political choices for the electors. Burke's letter to the Sheriffs of Bristol is a *locus classicus* for the trustee principle of elective representation. It is supported by Hobbes's principle that representation is agency: if you elect someone to represent you, you empower him or her to act for you as if he or she were you. Insofar as anything can become a political issue, you have given your elected representative a political version of general power of attorney.

This is a potentially alarming notion. It can also be seen as having the benefit of making people think carefully about how they exercise their electoral franchise. Defenders of the trusteeship theory cherish a picture of wise, benevolent and, above all, trustworthy gentlemen (and ladies) dispassionately determining what's best for the beneficiary, the electorate that entrusted the trustees with their duty of care—and pays them to perform it. The setting is a panelled boardroom or other such secluded sanctum. This is an ambivalent image, one suggesting either confidentiality and high-mindedness or secrecy and unaccountability. Two different experiences of misconduct detract from the first, beguiling picture: law societies having (or failing) to compensate clients for their lawyers' breach of trust; and states flouting the international law of trusteeship over dependent territories they have been awarded.

The whole idea is belied by the fact that, apart from matters *sub judice* (and, in municipal government, a few others relating to personnel and land use zoning), elected assemblies deliberate in public and their proceedings are minuted if not fully recorded. Secondly, political controversy "out of doors" and legislative debate are made inseparable by inquisitive media coverage and political party publicity machines. Some say that the putative-trustee image is negated by the facts of majority government, in which public policy decisions have been made and set—in uncured party and/or cabinet cement—before legislative debate and enactment. This is much less the case in the U.S., where separation of legislative and executive powers and Congress's bicameral "reconciliation" process can make for protracted (and leaky) debate. Apart from publicity stunts such as televised cabinet-meeting moments—psy as much as photo ops, with Ministers (or Secretaries) hanging on their leader's every word—cabinet decision-making is generally shielded from public scrutiny by cabinet confidentiality and solidarity. President Trump seems not to believe in either, inviting all and sundry—i.e., media and Congress persons—into policy meetings, in some of which he is seen and heard arguing with supporters as well as opponents. Some suspect that this occasional, uncharacteristic practice of transparency is a ploy, an attempt to conceal his habit of ignoring or flatly rejecting advice, however couched—including from his own appointees, some of whom seem to have been as casually selected as those of the contemptuous Roman Emperor Caligula.

At the other end of the representation theory spectrum is the delegation principle of election to office. It is all but impossible to uphold in cabinet government—or in any decision-making among realistic options for executive action. (Canada's Progressive Party loosely espoused it and elected 65 MPS in 1921; the party broke up in 1930, its more radical members joining the new CCF in 1932, and the remainder, small farmers and businessmen for the most part, amalgamating with the Conservatives in 1942 to form the Progressive-Conservative Party, elected to government in 1957-'63, 1979 and 1984-'93.) In its strictest version, elected representatives enter a legislative assembly armed with lists of dos and don'ts their electors expect them to follow religiously. These lists may be demands from those whose votes they courted more than others'; or compiled by candidates themselves as a platform of promises made to the electorate. Two prime examples of the latter are Newt Gingrich's "Contract with America" and Donald Trump's "big, beautiful" southern border wall. A well-known case of an overriding (and perhaps unconstitutional) commitment is the Grover Norquist pledge, whereby Republican members of the U.S. House of Representatives signed away (they seemed to believe) their right, under any circumstances, to vote for any tax increase whatsoever. Some found the courage to put their oath of office before any electoral rewards they might reap by swearing fealty to one political lobbyist and his one big idea.

The usual welter of issues facing voters makes it difficult to say with certainty how a democratically elected government is betraying its mandate. Campaign promises are generally understood and accepted as good intentions whose fulfillment hinges on circumstances, including what will be "discovered" to have been done, or left undone, by the previous government. This proviso also affects (if anything, more so) members and parties that want to be the people's delegates—unless they are single-issue politicians whose policy commitment is personal and not solely by delegation. Whether or not they are (or have been by others) committed to pressing forward on one salient or narrow front, they are the ones who will be ignored, and betrayed, by the ways and wiles of the institution in which they chose to seek office. If they (improbably) rise to an executive position, they are soon disabused of any notion that, before all else, they can do whatever they promised or were delegated to do.

— CHAPTER 7 —

Equal and Effective Representation

Most Americans have never heard of William Nicholas "Bill" Vander Zalm, B.C.'s 28th Premier (1986-'91) and a faint, faraway foretaste of President Donald John Trump. Like him, Bill married a woman from the former Yugoslavia—and has remained so for 65 years. Unlike the Trump family, the Vander Zalms kept their foreign surname—Bill had difficulty with "British," calling British Columbia Britis Columbia, a pronunciation problem that never lost him any political support.

Bill's political career was terminated by the disgrace of his using the office of Premier to consummate the sale of his theme park, Fantasy Gardens, not to mention the humiliation of broadcast recordings of his haggling with the sale's broker, the frightful Faye Leung. Nevertheless, he has retained a presence in B.C. politics. He re-emerged, two decades after his fall from grace, as the demi-god and demagogue of the 2010-'11 anti-HST campaign. He had always been a populist and small-business evangelist, his ineradicable persona even when his many horticultural ventures had earned him millions and after mounting to the top of the B.C. political heap. He ran for the provincial Liberal

Party leadership—partly, and unsuccessfully, on his reputation for welfare-bum-bashing when mayor of Surrey, Vancouver's largest suburb. His style was set early on by its municipal politics, long dominated by characters straight out of *Glengarry Glen Ross*. His populism had nothing to do with calls for social justice. It was a strictly political egalitarianism, as in the Reform Party's unbending pursuit of an elected Canadian Senate with equal representation for each province, following the U.S. example.

As Premier, the Zalm (pronounced ZAM! as in a Marvel comic book) did two things he promised would bring more power to the people— by which he meant not giving them additional power *in* government but making government power more attentive to them and, he hoped, vice versa. The first was a political tease supposed to bring about more intensive as well as more extensive citizen input through the creation of new provincial regions to be administered by new ministries of state, another layer of government—a prospect always unlikely to arouse much enthusiasm. His new regions were bundles of places and portions of places that were going to give their residents a new focus for their (newly acquired) common concerns. How this artificial apparatus was going to promote citizen participation and prosperity was never made clear. In truth, the whole experiment never got very far off the drawing-board; but several cabinet ministers now had to answer additional questions, in both press scrums and the House, about their new, ill-defined responsibilities.

Vander Zalm's other contribution to political equalizing has been more durable. In 1987 his government appointed an electoral boundaries commission with one primary objective: elimination of multi-member constituencies. Justice Thomas Fisher's report, adopted by the legislature in 1988, redesigned the electoral map, recommending a 25% rule of allowable deviation from equal rep(resentation) by pop(ulation) for each constituency. Given B.C.'s geography, it was impractical to try to get any closer to strict rep by pop. As it was, "Bulky"-Stikine contained some 30,000 people (roughly 5,000 more than the average), spread out over one-fifth of B.C.'s very large area (a daunting travel prospect for its new MLA). Total assembly seats increased from 69 to 75. Atlin, long a kind of representational reserve for the few-hundred Nisga'a majority living there, was swallowed up by the new monster riding just described. The whole northwest area was electorally redrawn in 2009, ten years after the Nisga'as got treaty title to their lands.

The main equality argument for the appointment of the Fisher commission was that electors in multi-member ridings enjoyed more representation than those in single-member ones. This debate was overtaken by a proportional representation (PR) argument for multi-member ridings in which voters can make multiple choices on their ballot according to their preferential ranking of candidates. Whether the first two or three past the post win seats or the first, second and third choices of voters determine the outcome, in multi-member ridings voters tend to want to talk to the elected member they wanted to come first. (B.C. has had two- and three-member ridings before; and like an Olympic bronze-medallist, the third member was usually forgotten.) If voters want something done, they will probably choose a government member from their riding if its representation is split between government and opposition members (as has happened a few times in B.C.'s electoral history) or even from another riding.

An important aim for some PR advocates is election of people who represent a variety of minority interests and opinions in a constituency. Another objective has been, as it was for J.S. Mill in his *Considerations on Representative Government,* to loosen the partisan grip on voting and elect more people of great society-wide stature, "eminent persons," who would leaven the legislative lumpen. Their election could, however, have some undesirable results. Independently minded members are (like doctrinal minority parties) less inclined than mainstream party faithful to be willing to bargain or abandon some cherished principle in return for some effective socio-economic betterment power; and government formation could be a long, arduous process. The connection between electorates and their government could become more tenuous than it already is, because of constituency enlargement and bewilderingly multi-member election results—which would, on the other hand, increase the chances of a government member being elected. Unless some maximum allowable members per riding were stipulated, the 5% popular vote threshold could expand total House membership beyond the 95 foreseen in B.C.'s 2018 ProRep referendum—in which PR was defeated, partly because the ballot also asked voters to choose one of three different PR schemes, two of which had not been tried or tested in any jurisdiction.

— CHAPTER 8 —

Keeping Them Honest

Some say B.C. is Canada's California, although in terms of climate and culture, that only (sort of) applies to the southwest corner of the province—except that further east but at roughly the same latitude (in both senses of the word), there's the wine culture of the Okanagan Valley and the cannabis culture of some mountain valleys in the West Kootenays. Most of B.C.'s first colonists came by sea — immigrants and fortune-seekers, some of whom still wander in, by thumb, and stay. Many came from California in search of new gold in the Cariboo region. A notable one was Joseph Trutch. While working in California, he learned to treat aboriginals as sub-humans and brought that lesson to B.C. He held, among other public offices, that of the new province's first Lieutenant-Governor. (He was born in England and returned to die, knighted for his service to Crown colony and *British* Columbia.) A notably odd arrival was Bill Smith from Nova Scotia, who changed his name to Amor de Cosmos, became a journalist and then B.C.'s second Premier. It is said, not only in jest, that B.C. means Beyond Canada. Another California import is the "direct democracy" rights of initiative, recall and referendum.

The right to recall an MLA (approved by referendum as part of B.C.'s 1991 general election, and subsequently legislated) is heavily qualified and has worked only once, in what could be called a pre-emptive resignation. The MLA in question was discovered to be the author of testimonials, written as if from constituents thanking him for his service, that were published as letters to the editor of a local newspaper. A recall movement was started, which gained such momentum that he saw the proverbial writing on the wall and, anticipating the required number of signatures being gathered before the stipulated deadline, resigned. He was a physically imposing figure, so tall that when he stood in his place in debate, the Hansard TV crew had to make camera adjustments for "Hercules" (as they dubbed him). He had a fine voice, occasionally entertaining the House by singing a few bars from a Handel oratorio—of no relevance to the debate; he was just showboating (including musicological information for other members' edification).

Under Gordon Campbell, the Liberals made a campaign promise of a referendum on the aboriginal treaty process initiated by the previous NDP government. They kept that promise on attaining power in 2001, and got the kind of result it was presumed they were looking for—and then carried on doing what their NDP opponents and bitter rivals had been doing. It seems that Liberal Party leaders were more finely attuned to shifting currents of public opinion on this issue than their campaign rhetoric had indicated. The number and nature of the questions posed in the mail-in ballot were designed to exasperate voters and produce a low return. This treaty negotiation referendum process helped make the case for legislation, akin to the federal Clarity Act, requiring concision as well as clarity in the wording of referenda.

Eight questions were asked, all of them raising further questions about implications and ramifications. There were three legal challenges, all of them dismissed. One of them complained about lack of voter education and "the very limited time between the passage of the Treaty Negotiations Referendum Regulations and the date established for the issuance of voting packages" to all B.C. households, with an information brochure. For two months prior to the final return date of May 15, 2002, information centre operators assisted roughly 30,000 voters. The return of 763, 480 valid ballots, almost 36%, was not low by municipal election standards. But on what could have become a constitutional issue, 60% or more (if not the Scottish independence referendum's huge 85% turnout) could be deemed essential: the outcome of this particular B.C. referendum could have led to changes in its governmental structure and processes. A 40-60% return could have been divisive in a fragmenting way, in part because as well as there being non-apathetic abstainers, 10-20% of voters may have opted for a least bad ballot choice. The 85-95% yes vote is impressive, but that spread is an indicator of some difficulties presented by multi-pronged questions, for both voters and counters. In addition to abstention as an expression of rejection of the referendum or of some of its questions, there was scope for the inability of even well-informed voters to fully understand all questions, and for government "construction" of partial answers.

B.C.'s right of extra-parliamentary initiative—also approved in the 1991 election and then legislated; and, like the right of recall, hedged with conditions the law requires be met—will, if exercised and successful according to the rules, result in a referendum. The legislative assembly is sovereign (until dissolved for an election), and can choose to ignore or alter the "message" sent by an intervening referendum. Any government can claim a systemic mandate to ignore the legislative assembly and appeal directly, over members' heads, to the people at large; and there is also the singular power of a Prime Minister or Premier to ignore his own caucus and party. In any such scenario a party's electoral chances would probably drive a Premier or Prime Minister from office. (As described below, a Premier or Prime Minister can be ousted for much less.)

There are lots of examples of shrewd governments wasting opportunities, offered by representative democracy's rules and procedures, to extricate themselves from the consequences of their mistakes. One is the Campbell government's handling of the controversy created by its decision to replace B.C.'s duo of a provincial sales tax (PST) added to a federal goods and services tax (GST) with a single, federally administered tax that covered more items at a slightly higher rate (the harmonized sales tax or HST). The Campbell Liberals were accused of treachery, having denied they were even considering adoption of the HST and then, shortly after re-election as government, consummating a tax deal with the feds. They had some good fiscal arguments on their side, not to mention a hefty federal signing bonus. On the other side were some items hitherto exempt being taxable—and the perceived deceitful flip-flop. A grass-roots fire of anti-HST sentiment flared up, which was whipped into an inferno by the ever-vigilant comeback retiree Bill Vander Zalm, while the official opposition NDP played Cheshire cat from the sidelines.

The opportunity to contain the blaze came with a motion, referred to a standing committee of the House, to put the deal to debate and a vote of the full House. House debate may expose the government to lengthy and intense public scrutiny, and to the possibility of dissent and defections by government MLAs. The likely outcome was a government victory; but public acceptance of HST just because the House approved it could be grudging at best. Like all committees, this one's composition reflected that of the House membership; and rather than take a calculated risk and vote for the motion, the government majority did what the government wanted—or what it believed the government wanted. It was a predictable result, as was a widespread perception that the government's reputation for being an arrogant bully and its backbenchers "a bunch of sheep" had been reinforced.

Under the recall and initiative legislation (in some small part the brainchild of the aforementioned Vander Zalm when he was Premier), petitions were duly circulated and signed in every constituency by enough voters within the required time span to force a referendum choice between the HST and the PST-GST. Meanwhile, Premier Campbell had been compelled to resign by a cabinet revolt. Any effort in favour of the HST by Premier Christy Clark and her new-old cabinet was crippled by their need to distance themselves from the discredited Campbell regime and its "dirty deal" with the feds. (Non-NDP B.C. political parties have ties with either or both of the national Conservatives and Liberals. Christy Clark had "family" ties to the federal Liberals, but all non-NDP B.C. governments are conservative in outlook, and the national government was Conservative at the time. Ideology is not a factor here, and Prime Minister Stephen Harper had constitutional as well as partisan reasons to let the B.C. government stew in its own juices.) No longer an MLA—she returned to the House in a by-election—and elected leader by the party rank and file, Clark had to promise government adherence to the referendum result. The HST option went down to defeat, and the long, painful process of reinstating the PST began. To add to the misery, reneging on the deal with the feds entailed withdrawal of the sweetener, leaving a multimillion-dollar hole in the provincial budget and the sour taste of a twofold loss of bribe and face. Two years later, the Premier became a miracle worker by converting, in the course of the one-month election campaign of 2013, a 17-point opinion poll deficit into a larger Liberal government majority.

[Chapters 9, 10 and 11 cover the peaks, valleys and final demise of B.C.'s Social Credit Party and its rebirth as the Libcreds, and also how third parties can cut in and change the political dance from tango to cha-cha-cha to bossa nova.]

WALT KELLY'S POTLUCK POGO

Chapter 31

THE SPEAKER SPOKES

It becomes apparent
that thinking is a sucker's game—
You can't take it with you.

ON YO' MARKS! THE SECOND ROUND OF THE GREAT INTER-RATIONAL THINKIN' CONTEST IS AT HAND--- GO IT, CHAPS!
THIS ONE'S ASLEEP.
I IS NOT-- AN' EVEN IF I IS-- I KIN OUTDREAM THE BEST THINKIN' HE'S DONE SINCE 19-OUGHT-36.

HEY!
UMP

HOW MUCH LONGER'S THEM TWO GONE BE OUT THINKIN' EACH OTHER?
WULL, BOTH BOYS IS STILL FRESH AN' UNMARKED.. NOT A KNOCK DOWN YET-

ALBERT GUV HISSELF A NOSE BLEED HANDLIN' HIGH TYPE THOUGHTS BUT IT DON'T COUNT.
THINGS BEEN PERTY BUSY, HUH?
BUSY--!? WHOO! ALL OF US BEEN SO BUSY WE AIN'T HAD TIME TO THINK---
MOOM OVER.
UMP

I'SE GONE SCORE YOU BOYS FOR THIS ROUND--- WHAT'D Y'ALL THINK OF---?
I THUNK OF MAM'SELLE HEPZIBAH EATIN' JELLY BEANS..'BOUT A POUND.
I DID TOO-- ONLY I THUNK OF HER EATIN' MORE--A POUND AN'A HALF.
MMPS! 'PEAR LIKE ALBERT'S OUTSCORN YOU THERE--- HOW MANY JELLY BEANS IN A POUND?
LICORICE: 235--- OR RASP'B'RY: 417--- OR LEMON: 163---
AN' I THUNK OF ATLANTIC CITY.

ATLANTIC CITY IS ONLY ONE THING!
I THUNK OF IT BEIN' FOURTH OF JOOLY WEEKEND THERE--- YOU EVER SEE THE BEACH 'BOUT NOON?

HO HO! I THUNK OF A WHOLE MESS OF BABY SPIDERS!
BABY SPIDERS! WHOO! HARDEST THING OF ALL TO COUNT--- 'FRAID I GOTTA SCORE YOU BOYS 'BOUT EVEN!

I IS THINKIN' OF GRASS---ALL THE GRASS BLADES IN THE WORL'
I IS THINKIN' OF SAND---ALL THE SAND GRAINS EVERYWHERE.

I IS THINKIN' OF RICE---BOILED! FRIED! WILD! AN' WITH RAISINS.
I IS THINKIN' OF ALL THE BLACK EYE PEAS IN THE SOVEREIGN SOUTH!

I IS THINKIN' OF STRING UPON STRING OF HOT DOGS AN' AN' AN'--
I IS THINKIN' OF POP CORN---ALL WHAT'S ALREADY POPPED---AN' ALL WHAT'S POPPIN' NOW -POP-POP-POP-POP
POP-POP-POP-POP-POP POP-POP-POP-POP
MAKE HIM STOP POPPIN' CORN--HE'S MAKIN' A FARCE OUTEN OUR THINKIN' CONTEST.
WITH BUTTER
AN' SALTS

IF HE GONNA RUN UP A BIG SCORE BY JES' MENTAL POPPIN' CORN AN' COUNTIN' EACH POP... I'SE GONE THINK OF SPRING FROGS—
POP POP POP POP

PEEPIN' THEY LI'L' HEARTS OUT IN THE APRIL EVE... PEEP PEEP PEEP PEEP PEEP PEEP PEEP PEEP
POP POP POP POP POP POP POP POP POP POP

PEEP PEEP PEEP PEEP PEEP PEEP PEEP PEEP PEEP PEEP PEEP PEEP PEEP PEEP PEEP
POP POP POP POP POP POP POP POP POP POP POP POP PEEP POP POP POP POP POP PEEP

COME BACK HERE! HE'S POPPIN' SMALLER AN' SMALLER AN' BESIDES HE USED ONE OF MY PEEPS! HEY, YOU JUDGES!
POP PEP POP POO POO PAH POOT PA

— CHAPTER 9 —

The Vander Zalm Discontinuity

In 1991 the B.C. Liberal Party vaulted from a condition of morbidity to official opposition and government-in-waiting status. There had been no Liberal MLA in the B.C. House since Gordon Gibson's departure in 1979. For 40 years there were only two serious contenders for provincial government power: Social Credit and the CCF-NDP. Liberals and Conservatives were regularly reduced to five or fewer seats, or none at all. The only Conservative MLA of note (elected as a Socred then re-elected twice as a Conservative) in this period was George Scott Wallace, an Oak Bay GP, who was an independent in the positions he took, even though he was the leader of his party. It has long been moribund, in spite of brief polling bumps under new and soon-forgotten leaders Derrill Warren, Vic Stephens and John Cummins.

The new 17-member Liberal caucus contained four MLAs who had previously held elective public office—in the Yukon Territory Legislative Assembly, on the White Rock City Council, Delta Board of School Trustees and Delta Parks Commission, and Vancouver Parks Board. Most of these newcomers to provincial politics never expected to be elected, and some appeared to wish they had not been. As in any election, voters were looking at both individual candidates and their party label; in this case it had been so long since a Liberal MLA spoke and was quoted on his party's policies that, in the usual dearth of interest in party "literature," most Liberal voters went for someone who was seen as centrally located between the same old ideological warriors. They did in large numbers, the Liberal popular-vote gain matching the Socreds' loss almost exactly—and in a first-past-the-post system, allowing the NDP's 2% loss to yield them a 132% gain in seats. Many attributed the election result to the celebrated Gordon Wilson zinger that skewered the other two in the three leaders' TV debate. Socred Premier Rita Johnston got into a slanging match with NDP leader Mike Harcourt, and as they were catching their breath the Liberal leader landed the following gob-smacker: "And that, ladies and gentlemen, is why nothing gets done in the B.C. legislature."

This unforeseen change in B.C.'s political landscape was prepared five years earlier when Bill Vander Zalm came back in out of the cold—to be warmly embraced by…? The Social Credit Party establishment didn't welcome him back as a replacement for retiring Premier Bill Bennett. Cabinet heavyweights Grace McCarthy, Jim Nielsen and Brian Smith were uneasy about competition from a former colleague not noted for being a team player. But party convention delegates loved him, and he led from first to last ballot. The government of William II was looking shopworn, and the party faithful were looking for a knight whose armour didn't squeak.

Future Socred MLA Kim Campbell—last on the convention's first ballot but seven years later the first female Prime Minister of Canada—bowed out with a speech warning the party that it should not choose style over substance. During the 1993 federal election campaign, newly anointed PM Campbell made some refreshingly candid and substantially risky comments that contributed to her own political demise—and, as collateral damage spread over ten years, demise of the Progressive-Conservative Party of Canada. A peculiar Canadian hybrid with a lifespan of roughly 60 years, for a quarter of which it was the national government, the P-Cs were led by men of great personal integrity (notably Robert Stanfield) but lacking in the killer instinct—until PM Brian Mulroney (1984-'93) taught the party to do whatever was needed to win and retain power, a lesson some party stalwarts found indigestible.

The truism about B.C.'s persistently polarized politics is not the whole truth, but it is worth repeating. One could say the same about the long Grits-and-Tories seesaw in the Atlantic provinces, but it lacked the ideological fervour of the B.C. split. It was, until the coming to power (for one term) of the NDP in Nova Scotia, a seemingly endless Tweedledum-and-Tweedledee affair and more about patronage than policy. Prince Edward Island politics are, as befits a province whose population is so small that it makes Rhode Island look like a mega-state, a family argument, now joined by the Green Party—which recently sent a Green MP to Ottawa from New Brunswick. The political left on the Pacific coast has strong labour union ties, bedevilled by a tradition of bolshie anarcho-syndicalism among some workers in B.C.'s three main industries, now in various forms of retreat: commercial fishermen (sorry, fishers), loggers and miners. This Wobbly sentiment came north with miners from the U.S.

A two-part event in the early 1950s ended several years of B.C. political fluidity and coalition government. First was B.C.'s importation of Alberta Social Credit political "philosophy" in the person of the very Reverend E.G. Hansell. Second, following a Liberal-Conservative coalition government's defeat in 1952, was rapid absorption of many old-line Grits and Tories into the Social Credit Party, under its leader ex-Tory W.A.C. Bennett. He shrewdly dropped from his party platform all but the populist element in Socred doctrine, and scared an electorally useful number of voters into believing that his CCF opponents—more Christian than socialist, but neither religiously so—were godless Marxists and barbarians at the gate.

Bennett dumbfounded everyone when he created a government-run ferry system that drove Canadian Pacific Railway Co. (whose service was quite inadequate for the growing main-route traffic volumes), not unwillingly, out of all but the coastal freight business. His *coup de main* was, in effect, the nationalization (in provincial form) of a private-sector company that was the owner-operator of both Vancouver's transit system and the electric power grid for the almost one million people living in B.C.'s lower mainland. B.C. Electric had no place in his vision of a greater British Columbia, which he intended to build on exploitation of its natural-resource-rich hinterland. Emulating Canada's pre-eminent founding father John A. Macdonald, Bennett used his government to direct economic growth—above all, through B.C. Hydro, a Crown corporation he created to harness B.C.'s abundant water resources for electric power generation and to manage its province-wide distribution. Another key to "opening up the province" was a northern-oriented road-and-rail transportation strategy, supervised where the rubber hit the road by his flamboyant Minister of Highways, "Flying Phil" Gaglardi. The Premier's anti-CCF, free-enterprise supporters were blindsided. Some said that B.C. Electric CEO Dal Grauer was driven to his death by the shock of Bennett's actions. They were taken as much against Vancouver's elite, who never admitted to voting Socred and publicly mocked the party, as they were for a bigger and better B.C.

Under Bennett's son, Social Credit was a vociferous free-enterprise party, professing to be fiscally prudent managers of the taxpayers' money. They had long ago cut ties with the original social credit movement and its guru "Major" Douglas's monetary and wealth distribution theories, which mixed the major's business experience with the writings of A.R. Orage, associate of guild socialist G.D.H. Cole, and a half-baked precursor of J.M. Keynes's work on a better economic balance between production and consumption. Calling social credit a theory, an ideology or a movement can be misleading. In the interwar years the Social Credit League had loosely affiliated "chapters" in the U.K., Canada, Australia and New Zealand; but as a policy set or platform, the party defined itself according to its various national and sub-national settings, and used different names (e.g., New Zealand Democratic Party). Quebec's Ralliement des Créditistes du Canada won 26 seats in the 1962 federal election. Its leader, Réal Caouette, was a small-town Chrysler dealer who took brief political advantage of "Pepsi" (Quebec nickname for Americanized petit bourgeois and country hicks) resentment against political party and other elite establishments. Was he, like Bill Vander Zalm, a provincial "character"—or, in a U.S. setting, flyover-country inhabitant—and partial foretaste of the Donald, and will he also flame out and take "his" party down with him? Social Credit was intermittently leftish- or rightish-radical in practice, and doctrinally opposed to central bank power. In the Great Depression, Alberta Premier William "Bible Bill" Aberhart (a radio evangelist) issued provincial "funny money" in defiance of the Bank of Canada. B.C. Premier W.A.C. "Wacky" Bennett put public enterprise in charge of "commanding heights" of the province's energy and transportation infrastructure. And under him the Socreds won a long string of elections as the party of small business and hard-working "little people"—big business had nowhere else to go. Other than in Alberta and British Columbia, a party calling itself Social Credit has never formed government.

• • • • •

Something not entirely unexpected but politically exciting happened in 1986, the year of B.C.'s Expo party. The province's giddy mood had an effect on the Social Credit leadership convention, and the party's grass roots decided they should lift its spirits, just as residents and visitors to B.C.'s biggest bash (until the 2010 Winter Olympics) were lifting their glasses. Seeing Pat McGeer on the campaign trail during Expo '86 revealed a lot about the changing nature of B.C.'s natural governing party or coalition. Sitting outside in one of the beer gardens installed for the world's fair—a double first for B.C.—I saw McGeer, one of the cleverest (and most arrogant) figures in B.C. political history, pushing his way through the throng, with a couple of aides trawling for votes. He was a brain specialist in UBC's faculty of medicine, and like most doctors he knew what was best for you. He was not a happy warrior in the autumn of 1986. His bemused sneer said it all: why am I here pressing the flesh (albeit hurriedly) of these festive peasants? He need not have bothered. For his efforts, he was the sole Socred notable to be defeated. One view is that he didn't care anymore, having lost his zest for political battle after over 25 years of mixing it up with an inferior sort of person, in both government and opposition. The first thing McGeer did after the Socred victory in December 1975, as minister responsible for ICBC, was order a big increase in what he said were taxpayer-subsidized auto insurance premiums. He answered his critics with "Let them eat cake" comments about getting vehicles that cost less to insure, riding a bike or taking the bus. Blue-collar supporters who had festooned their pickups with "NDP is NDG [No Damn Good]" before the election angrily switched to a new bumper sticker, "Stick It in Your Ear McGeer!"

Whatever their motivation, Socreds chose to go into the 1986 fall election, as Expo ended in a warm glow, led by the charismatic Zalm. He was part celebrity idol, with his movie-star good looks, part evangelist, and part shrewd man of the people—and of the soil, with his sturdy gardener's hands and signature pipe. He was easily depicted as a cartoon character, and a bit of a charlatan, a mixture of Elmer Gantry and Mark Trail—a comparison that dates me, but it fits the era of his political flowering. He had been around the political block, and did not arrive at the top of B.C.'s greasy pole on charm alone, or style without substance. For example, when he was Minister of Municipal Affairs, he was invited to address a public meeting in the town of Langford, turbulent heart of Victoria's western communities. He stood and spoke—sans notes, lectern or flunkies—on the vexed topics of amalgamation and incorporation, fielded some unfriendly questions, and left the impression that he was in command of both the occasion and his portfolio.

During his absence from the legislature, and another foray into municipal politics (a bid to become mayor of Vancouver), the Social Credit Party moved further into the political mainstream, becoming more urbane as well as less socially conservative. In 1975, when its second (Bennett Jr.) phase began and Vander Zalm was first elected to the provincial legislature, the party acquired MLAs from a more urban, more liberal Liberal elite, in particular Garde Gardom, Pat McGeer and Allan Williams; also Jack Davis, a former federal Liberal cabinet minister. Progressive-Conservative lawyer Brian Smith was recruited in 1979. Their political careers representing affluent suburbs went back, in the case of McGeer, to 1962. All five served under Bill Bennett in major cabinet posts.

The Davis and Smith stories help explain what held Social Credit together and what tore it apart. Jack Davis is remembered as a Rhodes Scholar because Bennett demanded Davis's resignation from cabinet over a minor but fraudulent air travel expense claim, then laconically dismissed the Davis camp's contention that the government could ill afford to discard one of its few intellectual luminaries: "Only in America, my friends." That was in 1978. Davis returned to cabinet, and died serenely in office. He enthralled his staff with his expansive, visionary ideas while around him the Vander Zalm administration crumbled. Ten years after Davis's expulsion from cabinet, Brian Smith, the Zalm's Attorney-General, resigned, citing Premier's Office interference with the customary independence of the province's chief law enforcement officer. Was this another foretaste of the Trump effect on government—and of the badly managed resignation of PM Trudeau's A-G and Minister of Justice? While doing some Hansard research in the Socred caucus offices, I saw Smith storm in with bed hair, one side of his shirt collar up, a thunderous countenance, and his pipe gripped (upside down) in his teeth—and smoking, or maybe it was coming out of his ears. The bed Brian finally decided to get out of was the Socred one. Premier Vander Zalm may have felt that there was no room in cabinet for two pipe puffers, or more likely, feared the proximity of a rival (second at the convention) for the leadership.

Davis, McGeer and Smith were the brains trust of Socred governments after the first, "Wacky" Bennett era. But they were short on political affect—too remote from the party base, lacking the common touch perhaps, or too fastidious for the same old slugfest between Social Credit worthies and "godless socialists." Fortunately for Socred cabinet ministers who were federal Tories, Mulroney's victory in 1984 gave them a safe haven after departing the Vander Zalm regime. Two given lucrative employment—some say sinecures—in Ottawa were Smith and Jim Hewitt (chairman of CN Rail and the Farm Credit Corporation, respectively). The federal escape hatch, with golden parachute, was firmly closed for old Grits like Davis and McGeer.

· · · · ·

Some of the Socred MLAs elected for the first time in the Zalm's 1986 victory were regime indicators. Although he's a Roman Catholic, the party maintained its grip on the Fraser Valley Bible Belt. He attracted candidates in other parts of the province who believed that government should be based on Christian principles. The second member for Cariboo (Alex Fraser's running-mate) was Rev. Neil

Vant, boilermaker, prospector and Anglican priest. Perhaps thinking it was required of a ranch-country representative, he often wore western garb; but it seemed to make him both physically and mentally uncomfortable. Neither Fraser, a multi-term MLA, nor Dave Zirnhelt, the new (1991) MLA for Cariboo South and a heavy-horse rancher, apparently felt the need to look like cowboys. Terry Huberts, a veterinarian, was elected second member for Saanich and the Islands, behind Mel Couvelier, also a first-term MLA but a ten-year mayor of Saanich who became Vander Zalm's first and only Minister of Finance. I have a vivid memory of him springing up the steps on his way to the first sitting of the 34th parliament, wearing one of his haberdashery's finest suits and a Liberal red rose in his lapel—it should have been between his teeth. Huberts ran as an evangelical Christian, and his maiden speech was devoted less to his riding, the usual core of such speeches, than to his religious beliefs and the role they would play in his conduct as an MLA.

Another sort of unusual maiden speech (Liberal, 1992) waxed philosophical. Plato, the new member said, "asserted" that one of the "fundamental features of a democracy…[is] that it is virtuous." He added, more Platonically, that it must be led by the wise, among whom he counted his new colleagues in the legislature—all of them. The shine soon wore off that shinola. His excitability got the better of him, and he lashed out at hecklers: "The fact is that the Minister of Employment has lied to this House; the Minister of Education has lied to this House; the plumed parrot [Mike Farnworth, still an NDP MLA and again a cabinet minister] has lied to this House." Not surprisingly, the Chair felt compelled to interrupt him. He refused to withdraw "lied," saying he felt "compelled to withdraw from the chamber"—which, after three times of asking for a withdrawal, the Chair would order him to do. He used unparliamentary language again, in debating the government's defence of a deal made by B.C. Hydro with the (U.S.) Bonneville Power

Administration. But he was not alone in thinking that B.C. was being conned by Uncle Sam (called Sam Slick by Thomas Haliburton in his pre-Confederation stories about a Yankee clockmaker peddling his wares in Canada's Atlantic region).

Both Huberts and Vant made it into the Zalm cabinet, as some old warhorses were replaced by loyal lightweights. Huberts was one of the most tight-lipped ministers ever to defend his estimates (ministry money votes) in B.C.'s House. He would not (or was unable to?) divulge anything of substance about his responsibilities and treated the name of one of his portfolios as if it were a state secret—it was one of the Zalm's ministries of state, whose point and function nobody could understand.

Dave Parker, the MLA for Skeena, was a high-grading forest industrialist and as such a controversial choice to be Minister of Forests. The Zalm's first choice, Jack Kempf, lasted six months. He had strong views, which he had been declaiming as an MLA since 1975; but he and they were incompatible with the administrative complexities of running a major government department. It was as if Vander Zalm had yielded to a politically unwise predilection for people who, like himself, shot from the lip. Kempf left in a huff to sit as an Independent.

John Reynolds was a surprise choice for Speaker of the House—he had (federal) parliamentary experience; the surprise was that he did not go straight into cabinet. The Hansard relationship with him was awkward. Ignoring years of research on legislative television undertaken by then chief of Hansard Garth Gislason, Reynolds offered a trial run to some videographers in his constituency, whom he commissioned to make a movie of the legislature at work, starting with our offices. Suffice it to say, everyone was thankful the amateur efforts of that hapless group were terminated when Reynolds was appointed Environment minister in 1989—a move that turned into a real surprise. It was widely assumed that, with his business background, Reynolds would be industry-friendly. However, the air pollution regulations he announced caused pulp-and-paper companies to squeal in pain.

With Vander Zalm at the helm, the Socred cruise ended in a *Costa Concordia* grounding. A more apt metaphor than one drawn from foreign vessels or overworked wrecks like the *Titanic* would be B.C. Ferries' *Queen of the North*. Its sinking did not occur on Vander Zalm's watch, nor could it be hung around any government neck; B.C. Ferries had been quasi-privatized by a later Liberal administration. Blame for the *Queen*'s tragic loss could be laid at many Ferry Corporation doors. But the combination of paying scant attention to navigation in treacherous waters, inexperience and/or negligence on the bridge and a lovers' quarrel fits the facts of the fate of the last Socred regime. Tourism minister Bill Reid earlier (and presciently) summed up the official reaction to the prospect of any dire situation: "We have been assured that the eventuality of such an outcome is an unlikely possibility of certainly happening." Old hands headed for the lifeboats, and few were left who had not been invited into the wardroom (also known as the officers' mess).

What happened after the Vander Zalm honeymoon—a series of photo ops (many with native Indian communities and organizations) of no policy import—was a creeping disaster, as Social Credit lost every single by-election. The "eventuality" that did for the Zalm was the Fantasy Gardens debacle, a stunningly improper use of the Premier's Office to complete one last big deal. The Donald has no qualms about using the Oval Office in the same way. Could he have somehow learned from the Zalm's experience that blatant shamelessness is the better way to go and excuses anything? Trump: "I'm honestly free of shame." A-G Barr: "That's all very well, but you're blowing *my* cover when doing *your* bidding." Vander Zalm was judicially reproved, and had to retract an injudicious attack in his book on Justice Hughes's inquiry judgment. He escaped any criminal conviction, but there was never a satisfactory explanation for the brown-paper envelopes full of thousands of dollars that passed between him and the Taiwanese purchaser of his theme park.

East of the Rockies, B.C. is often seen to be a political loony-bin, its political debate now caught by Covid in the Zoom-doomed paws of legislative TV's Looney Toons deep frieze. Seasoned observers see in B.C.'s governance an underlying competence and stability. However, the province's reputation for solid administration beneath the partisan froth took a severe beating as the last Social Credit cabinet turned on itself and committed political hara-kiri. The sputtering torch passed from the belly of the beast to Rita Johnston, Minister of Transportation and Highways and then Canada's first female Premier. (PM Kim Campbell made it a double first for B.C. Does that mean women in Canadian politics are condemned to be always the charladies of governmental messes made by men?) Rita was the fall gal; but compared to her cabinet colleagues, her background as the manager of a trailer park was more useful in leading the remains of the Vander Zalm government than any of theirs. The Zalm was relegated to his party's back bench, as the first member for Richmond. He bravely suffered humiliation at the hands of Speaker Stephen Rogers, who revenged himself on the Zalm for being dropped from cabinet in favour of new blood, in spite of his many years of legislative service and membership in Bill Bennett cabinets, with these words: "What possible point of order is that member for Richmond rising on now?" It was B.C.'s Death of a Salesman—but the leading man remained in the wings, rehearsing his lines for a reprise.

— CHAPTER 10 —

Nanaimo Bars the Way

When he was mayor of Vancouver, Mike Harcourt was widely regarded as Mr. Nice Guy, a reputation that helped him lead the NDP to victory in the 1991 general election and accompanied him throughout his tenure as Premier (November 5, 1991, to February 22, 1996). When they found out he really was one of Nature's nice guys—and we know what happens to them—his Liberal opponents smelled blood. One result of their hounding was his decision to resign shortly before the 1996 election because of what became known as Bingogate, for which it was eventually and generally acknowledged he and his government had no responsibility whatsoever. Harcourt said he was resigning to save his party. An additional and equally plausible reason is that he was fed up with the slings and arrows he was forced to endure because a long-buried non-governmental malfeasance had been exhumed as a full-blown political scandal.

Incoming NDP Premier Glen Clark had made a leadership campaign promise to establish a full public inquiry into "all NCHS activities and any other matters relating to gaming and the handling of charitable funds in the province." Judge Nathan Nemetz was chosen to head it; five years later it had turned into the Murray Smith commission, which was shut down by the new Liberal government because of rising costs, lengthy delays and the inability of key witnesses to testify. The inquiry's incomplete report was sealed from public view, and access to it was exempted from FOI (freedom-of-information) requests and applications.

The seeds of scandal were planted by Dave Stupich, CCF candidate, longtime NDP MLA (and MP), and founder of the non-profit NCHS (Nanaimo Commonwealth Holding Society). As the second word in its title suggests, it had a relationship with the Co-operative Commonwealth Federation, socialist predecessor of the NDP. He created the NCHS in the early 1950s to raise funds for the local CCF, and both grew in soil laid down by decades of conflict between coal-miners from Cumberland to Wellington and their baronial bosses. Calling the Dunsmuirs baronial is not mere class-warfare rhetoric. Chief among them was Robert Dunsmuir, who, like so many members of the Canadian branch of Scottish clans, had left his native land in straitened circumstances, grasped at New World chances, amassed great wealth, and then said "the working-class can kiss my ass." He and his son James spent the family coal fortune building castles in Victoria and its suburbs with which to lord it over other would-be colonial grandees. The E&N Railway, built by the Dunsmuirs to carry their coal from greater Nanaimo's coalfields to tidewater in Esquimalt, was indirectly paid for by generous government land grants.

The NCHS was a working-class charitable organization, and that function was the source of tribulation for the NDP and trial for Stupich. It raised a lot of money through bingo games whose popularity owed as much to the community charities they helped fund as to the prospect of winning. When it was revealed that Stupich, an accountant and keeper of the NCHS books, had diverted gaming proceeds to the NDP, a mixture of disbelief, dismay and disgust hit the proverbial fan. The fact that the NCHS had been explicitly started as a political fund-raiser did not help; nor did Stupich's reputation for unimpeachable integrity and self-restraint. In budget debate with Premier W.A.C. Bennett, who was his own Minister of Finance, Stupich was sharply critical but never attacked Bennett personally. If he had been quoting liberally from budget and related documents, he would invite me, as a Hansard editor, to use his files to verify the quoted material; and if it was after a morning sitting and he was going to lunch, he would say, "Help yourself," and leave the door open for me, and nobody else in his office. His being so open and trusting made it hard to believe he was not entirely trustworthy himself.

Was Stupich one of those otherwise upright persons with a moral blind spot? He may have sincerely believed that the NDP's political education role made it a charitable endeavour. It may have had something to do with his being an accountant doing income tax returns that deducted charitable and political donations, along with medical and educational expenses—all together, and altogether worthy and/or necessary parts of a full and decent life. But as a chartered accountant, he should have been alert to important legal distinctions in dealing with financial matters. And there was no ethical excuse for what amounted to theft of money from the charities that were meant to receive it. He seemed at the end to be genuinely bewildered by the public furor over Bingogate (much of it simulated for partisan effect)—perhaps he was just confused by advancing dementia.

As a democratic socialist, Stupich believed in greater distributive justice, in some redistribution of a nation's (or province's) wealth produced by collective societal effort. He also believed in charitable impulses and their societal value. The NCHS was ready-made for conversion of a person's pledge to fund, say, the Canadian Mental Health Association from being part of a "community chest" donation into something even bigger—by adding it to other, health-related "social services" commitments and thereby strengthening individual acts of charity. What could be better than having them work together towards a common, good end? That's all very well, some object, but having a menu from which to choose one's community-giving recipients is not the same as having one's choices subsumed by a political party's good social-welfare intentions—especially without express consent or a vote on each particular item of expenditure. In Stupich's defence, it could be said that good things bubbling up from a publicly operated well is more efficacious than having them trickle down from a few of the "great and the good," and makes for a steadier flow. Is it better to stand under a dribbling shower head or to sit in the soothing waters of a bidet? Either way, look out for "dirty hands" and douche-bags.

The Stupich case was a godsend for opponents of a party with a holier-than-thou-image. Premier Harcourt was not personally vulnerable to the charge of being an idol with feet of clay. He was just major collateral damage, part of the fallout from Bingogate. There's a lot to be said for being an ideological assortment, such as the B.C. Liberal Party, rather than one like the NDP, whose members value adherence to the party's foundational principles. A well-established, well-funded right-wing party can be confident its supporters have no other sensible option. The Canadian right fragmented briefly (1993-2002) but for largely regional reasons; and challenges to B.C. right-of-centre parties from the further right have sputtered and died. Whether its supporters want strict adherence to principle or compromise with practical reality, the left wing in power always disappoints some of them. Its one-time election-day supporters have a roving eye and a history of wandering over the ideological map. The NDP's campaign advantage of one united party for all elections, national and provincial (and as a farm team in some municipal ones), is undercut by everybody in the whole party being blamed for blunders committed by any party member anywhere in the country.

There was no evidence that any Nanaimo-area MLA or MP, or anyone anywhere else, who may have somehow benefited from NCHS funds knew anything about what Stupich was doing. Premier Harcourt appointed respected forensic auditor Ron Parks to look into the Bingogate affair. As any opposition party would do in similar circumstances, the Liberals said that nothing less than a full public inquiry headed by a judge would satisfy people. The NDP knew that such an inquiry could last into the next general election campaign, unearthing in the process all sorts of possibly damaging material that had nothing to do with Bingogate. If political pressure is unremitting, and the "authors" of their authority (per Thomas Hobbes) insist, democratic governments will submit as gracefully as they can. But they will also feel "obliged" to remind public opinion, and its partisan enablers, that they will have to accept their insistently desired inquiry's conclusions (which may exonerate the government) and the inquiry's cost, which will be paid from the public purse. In a case of misconduct in the post-NDP Liberal government's sale of B.C. Rail assets to CN Rail, taxpayers paid the legal costs of two ministerial aides who pleaded guilty—giving the NDP a further cause with which to avenge the long agony of Bingogate.

Harcourt's resignation came six months after he had to undergo debate on the estimates of the Office of the Premier (June 29, 1995, afternoon sitting), the occasion for a more than usually gruelling experience. After repeated jabs from official opposition members, it was the turn of minor-party and independent members. Harcourt was put through the same old wringer by Reform's Jack Weisgerber. The unkindest cut of all was Independent David Mitchell's *schadenfreude*, conveying his "compassion" for the Premier's "self-inflicted predicament."

Why didn't Harcourt tough it out? One answer is the powerful myth that tells us the king must die in order for the tribe to live another cycle. When the country's tom-toms say a Prime Minister must make way for somebody else, the 1922 Committee of the U.K.'s Conservative and Unionist Party tells him to go—and that includes the redoubtable Mrs. Thatcher. All political parties analyze public opinion polls, in search of a new name to pull the party over the top in the next election before voters find out that there is not as much behind the face as they were led to believe.

The 1996 B.C. NDP leadership convention chose one of the two young "pit bulls" who had harried the Vander Zalm government in legislative debate. Moe Sihota, the other attack dog, was under investigation by the B.C. Law Society and therefore out of cabinet and out of the running. Runner-up Corky Evans enjoyed a lot of rank-and-file support, partly because he sounded as if he would be, like Harcourt, an emollient Premier. The winner was Glen Clark, whose street-fighter reputation was based on his pre-political life as business agent for the ironworkers' union and on his having always lived in his working-class constituency. He turned out to be a frustrated ironworker with an edifice complex— as in sleek, catamaran car ferries that would pare precious minutes off travel time to and from Vancouver Island, and help restore B.C.'s shipbuilding industry. His performance as official opposition critic of Mel Couvelier, Socred Finance minister, had already softened his pit-bull image. Their night-sitting debates turned into amiable fireside chats, pretending high-finance tradecraft with breezy talk of stock market upticks and currency basis points. Did they presage his post-political surprise, a leap into upper-management employment with B.C. billionaire businessman (and philanthropist) Jim Pattison?

As Premier, Clark began with one essential ingredient of all success: luck. The NDP won a squeaker in 1996, losing seats (as expected) but retaining a majority—even as they lost in percentage of the popular vote; opposition support was too heavily concentrated in a handful of lower mainland constituencies. That, and an under-reported "fudge-it budget" deficit, embittered the Liberals for another five long years. It wasn't enough that Clark's government dug itself into a deep politico-fiscal hole in just about every aspect of its fast-ferry decision and program. The Liberals piled on with a smear campaign based on a hint of (unproven) impropriety in Clark's relationship with a neighbour who built him a deck but did not receive, as alleged, any return favour in regard to the casino licence bid of an associate. Video of a night police "raid" on the Premier's house sealed his fate. Would such a thing have happened if he lived in an up-market part of Vancouver, in some leafier suburb?

· · · · ·

The NDP has faith, albeit a secular one; like all political parties, it has hope; and it has, as its defining virtue, charity. The story of Dave Stupich shows that politics and charity make strange bedfellows. His mistake was to believe, as many apparently do, that charity is a political virtue. He took that to mean not only that charity is political—as it is, in spite of most charitable people sincerely disavowing any political motive—but also that political action is a form of love, which is what charity is in its original religious sense. A short, sharp reply is that politics is not about any virtue, but about Machiavelli's *virtù*. The added "e" means emotional excess.

In an excess of enthusiasm, during the trysting season between jousting sessions, NDP Premier Dave Barrett made a speech in which he said to leading Quebeckers: "Let's make love politically." It was 1975, and the weed smoke of flower power was still in the air. He was offering a west coast, hash-mash alternative to PM Trudeau's hard-nosed handling of Quebec sovereigntists and separatists. Most Canadians have travelled some four or five disillusioning decades past Barrett's effusion. However, what became a state funeral for NDP leader Jack Layton—on the morrow of the party's 2011 replacement of the Liberals as official opposition in the House of Commons, an election "victory" whose architect he was—dissolved into an NDP love-in. The theme of those who spoke (at great length) was generosity. Some were clergy from a full spectrum of religious belief. They should have thought of Job: in addition to generosity's recipients, fate and the gods will find a way to punish the generous. One speaker addressed Prime Minister Harper directly, and the PM's body language said it all: who are these people, and why are they using this bully pulpit to publicly shame me into some kind of conversion?

— CHAPTER 11 —

Interregnum and Restoration, Again

If anything was better than the dreaded NDP and its (alleged) anti-business bias, and Social Credit was heading for the rocks, why not take a chance on a motley crew of Liberals? The NDP was expected to win in 1991; the only question was by how much. Despairing Socred voters, feeling betrayed by both Vander Zalm and his party critics, saw in the Liberals a long shot to prevent an NDP landslide—and, more importantly, a non-socialist alternative that might support what was left (or rather, right) of Social Credit Party MLAs. The floating voters who saw them as an intriguing third choice, a chance for truly centrist and moderate government, embodied the Gilbert and Sullivan quatrain from *Iolanthe*: "Every boy and every gal/that's born into this world alive/is either a little Liberal/or else a little Conservative"—except that they were both, and thought they saw in the resurrected Liberals a lever with which to prise apart the Laocoon-like figures fixed in the statuesque struggle of B.C. provincial politics, and perhaps knock them off their plinth. The handful of returning Socred MLAs were called the Seven Dwarves—without their leader Rita Johnston, who was of course christened No Snow White. Four defected, enough to make them an officially recognized party caucus, and renamed themselves the B.C. Reform Party. Two others retired. Cliff Serwa, representing the Okanagan heartland of Social Credit (officially as an Independent), was the only one who kept the faith; he carried the Socred banner until retiring as an MLA before the party's 1996 electoral elimination.

The Liberals added more than one new dimension to their political party as a "big tent," a self-characterization of the Liberal Party everywhere in Canada. The B.C. Liberals owed their new lease on life to among others: a United Church minister mentally living in the Saskatchewan of NDP icon Tommy Douglas; the author of the definitive biography of Socred mega-Premier W.A.C. Bennett; a former chair of the Vancouver Parks Board, remembered only for his alacrity in resigning his seat to make way for a former mayor of Vancouver seen as the true leader of a new B.C. anti-socialist coalition; a community college law instructor whose legislative career was devoted to winning a property dispute for his in-laws; and a Canadian Army non-com rumoured to have entered the electoral fray on a bet with his CFB Chilliwack buddies. The second of these five became opposition House Leader, but left the party early when his perhaps too self-conscious attempts at statesman-like co-operation with the new government were rebuffed, including by some of his own caucus who had come for a fight. The last two ended up, one of them more or less willingly, in Independent wilderness. Rounding out the centrifugal forces in this disparate group were a cute and colourful young mother (who turned her office into a crèche and her leader into an adulterer), a manic academic, a furious flight instructor, a revanchist insurance salesman, an ebullient educator who became the longest-serving MLA, a transportation policy wonk, a telephone repairman who saw himself as an IT consultant to Hansard, and four moderately successful business people. Less than half of these 17 new MLAs were regular politicians in the sense of people who would survive candidate-vetting under normal competitive conditions.

If a party waits until its chances look better (because that will attract good candidates) before starting the selection process, it may be caught short by an early election call. If a long-marginal riding comes into play for the party, it may be stuck with a long-shot candidate already chosen in the absence of anyone else. Of course, it can—and increasingly does in a stable two-party situation—maintain a deep bench of highly qualified hopefuls; and it can force a constituency's long-standing choice to step aside for what party HQ thinks is a more attractive candidate (some instances of which have attracted unfavourable publicity). But when a lot of no-hopers gallop home, election night elation can turn into a hangover. The 1991-'92 Liberal headache group included leader Gordon Wilson, pole of the party's vault. On a centre-left-centre party platform—if anyone had bothered to read it, or cared—many winning Liberals were misplaced persons.

Once the Liberals replaced Gordon Wilson with Gordon Campbell, and settled into playing a consistently right-of-centre game, some low-value cards were shuffled out of the pack in advance of the next election. (The Liberal leadership contest featured three Gordons, none of them gay; but it did make for a very clannish-sounding event. Would there be a dance competition? Was it going to be decided by tossing the caber? Would the winner be chief tosser?) For the first time since WWII and Premier John Hart, sole power was within Liberal reach, and the party reserved one riding for star candidate and future A-G Geoff Plant. Just before the 1996 election the incumbent flounced out, trading in his Liberal marbles for the pebble of Independent in the far corner of the House, there joining other disgruntled MLAs (two Liberals and an NDPer). The latter was also a party reject, but for very different reasons and cast out from the great height of cabinet minister.

The Liberals came close in 1996, doubling their representation in the House—they beat the NDP in popular vote, but "wasted" votes in safe ridings. The potential for wayward members, although much reduced, was not eliminated. It should be said that a disciplined caucus is liable to be accused of mindless obedience; and second, that the larger the caucus the greater the chance of it including a few loose cannons. In the 1996 election the Liberal Party of B.C. acquired three new members who were not, by any measure, misfits. None of them were as undisciplined as one member of the Liberal back bench who will appear later in this chapter. But they sometimes disturbed the equilibrium of the official opposition ship by leaning a bit too far overboard in debate, by being a bit *outré* in the intensity of their opposition.

The first, the member for Okanagan-Vernon, was the least of them in this regard. She was a family doctor, and played her medical-practitioner ace along with a wild card that has been a perennial favourite among opposition members: the plight of a constituent (often a child) suffering from a rare disease requiring hugely expensive treatment denied her/him by the heartless health care system. She was compelling in debate, in part by wearing a shawl that was both elegant and made her look like a latter-day Florence Nightingale. What was potentially troubling for her party was certainly not that she might embarrass the government, but that she really meant what she said, that her appeal for special medical consideration was not a partisan debating tactic to be discarded if and when the Liberals formed government.

The second, Kevin Krueger, member for Kamloops—North Thompson, was from the same part of B.C.'s interior. He was a 20-year employee of the Insurance Corporation of B.C. who became Liberal attack dog in support of a secret ballot for union certification. He outdid any other member, past or present, in the foghorn category. His boom-box voice dominated House debate on the Raiwind affair, also known as Hydrogate. It broke early in the administration of NDP Premier Glen Clark, when B.C. Hydro chairman John Laxton was discovered peddling shares in an overseas venture of the Crown corporation and cutting cheques to Ali Mahmoud, one of its Pakistani partner's presumed representatives. The final report on the affair found Laxton to have been in a serious conflict of interest, for which he was fired—and replaced by Brian Smith, former A-G, chairman of CN Rail, and writer of the report.

Meanwhile, back at the legislative ranch, the Liberal opposition got stuck in. The main action took place in the Douglas Fir committee room, where gimlet-eyed Gary Farrell-Collins, dyspeptic demiurge of the Liberal Party's rebirth as the vanguard of B.C.'s anti-NDP forces, grilled Dan Miller, the minister responsible for B.C. Hydro. (This Liberal attack dog rebranded himself plain Mr. Collins on being appointed Minister of Finance in the new, 2001 Liberal government's mopping-up of the mess made by the NDP during its "ten terrible years" in office.) His real target was not Dan Miller but Moe Sihota, with whom Collins had clashed in debate of union-friendly Labour Code amendments. Collins was an awkward but grimly determined debater; Sihota, the silky Sikh, was contemptuously dismissive—as Miller could be too, which made him a convenient stalking-horse. There was more than righteously public-spirited indignation in Collins's demeanour as he strode down the corridor to resume nightly battle over Hydrogate and its Pakistani connection. Personal or political, his goal was that, one way or another, the Punjab was going to pay.

Krueger's part in this drama was played in the full House with its resonant acoustics, especially for those, like Krueger, who needed no artificial amplification. He seized any opportunity, whenever the subject of Raiwind and Mahmoud came up (or even if it didn't), to make his distinctive contribution to debate, bellowing "Whooo is Mahmoood?" No one seemed to know the answer, or would not attempt one. While Krueger's interjection was a rhetorical question, it was part of the whole affair becoming a scandal that for days the mysterious middleman was never properly identified nor, for that matter, his existence verified. Krueger's question was never answered in debate, but its occasional inclusion in the report was felt to be required because strict observance of the interjection rule would have been like ignoring a nuclear explosion. Its sheer decibel count made us ponder WHOOO IS MAHMOOOD? in the *Hansard* text. Like a graffiti artist tagging the walls, he was broadcasting a subliminal image of B.C.'s fair-maiden taxpayer being abducted by some wily oriental, dragged into the souk and ravished. The Djangoling undertone of racist xenophobia accompanying Krueger's drumbeat question warned other members to treat it like a roadside IED best left alone.

Another booming bravura performance by Krueger was his assault on the NDP government's plan to raise revenue by licensing more slot machines and gambling casinos. He rang all the changes on crime, addiction, mental breakdown and broken homes. It was enough to make a croupier cry. In the Liberal government's first three terms (2001-'13), during which Krueger was for a while Minister of Tourism and thereby somewhat responsible for tourist entertainment, casinos grew in size and number, and "problem gambling" increased.

It was a combination of alcohol, fatigue and annoyance that in midsummer session precipitated one of the strangest incidents in B.C. House history. It occurred during an evening sitting, one of many needed to accommodate Ted Nebbeling's merciless pursuit of the Forests minister during his ministry's estimates. The NDP minister was Dave Zirnhelt; Nebbeling (the member for West Vancouver—Garibaldi) was his Liberal official opposition critic. Fatigue brought on by his interrogation—and the dreadful prospect of it going on to ruin many beautiful summer evenings—may explain Zirnhelt's notorious outburst that a government can do whatever it wants just because it's the government. He did not say it in his bout with Nebbeling, but it could well have been nurtured, as a festering sore, during the torture of his unanswerable because incomprehensible questions, buried in rambling broken English, his command of which was poor in spite of his having been in Canada long enough to be twice elected mayor of Whistler. The result was numb despair for all concerned.

A trio of merry pranksters, the NDP's Sue Hammell and Joy MacPhail plus Liberal Bonnie McKinnon, came back to the House after dinner and drinks, and to its rescue. (As cabinet ministers, Hammell and Mac-Phail may have been trying to end their colleague's torment.) Most members were in a state of stupefaction, and didn't take particular notice of the three late arrivals, who snuck up behind Nebbeling and placed a vibrating dildo on his desk. It cannot be verified from the videotape what precisely diverted his gaze and for a moment halted his tirade. He reared back in understandable surprise, and then, with admirable aplomb, promptly resumed his inquisition of Zirnhelt. There was no comment on the discursus interrruptus from any member, including Nebbeling. There were guarded references in the press to a "mechanical toy." It was an event that deserved being marked by Hansard inserting (fittingly if not quite appropriately) a visual (and tactile) image in the shape of a pop-up in the gutter (so to speak) between pages. A certain *frisson* came with this incident because of Nebbeling's semi-closeted status—unlike that of concurrently serving and proudly gay NDP MLA Rev. Tim Stevenson.

None of the three occasionally eccentric Liberal MLAs highlighted here was as unruly a caucus member as McKinnon when she joined two NDP women in an attempt to disconcert a Liberal Party spokesperson. Krueger and Nebbeling became cabinet ministers; McKinnon and the party(ing) parted company, she became an Independent, and was defeated in 2001, when the Liberals came within two seats of a clean sweep. (Unlike the P-C Party, which was also reduced to two seats in the 1993 federal election, then bled to death from Reform, Canadian Alliance and finally the present Conservative Party's vampire bites, B.C.'s NDP recovered from its near-death experience.) Liberal victory in 2001 was as inevitable as anything can be in politics. One noteworthy phenomenon was the number of Socreds who came back to life in Liberal clothing—hence the party being labelled the Libcreds. In addition to some former party members and candidates, there were half a dozen who had been Social Credit MLAs, two of whom had held cabinet posts and were appointed to the first Liberal cabinet in over 50 years (Stan Hagen and Claude Richmond, along with former Socred MLAs Graham Bruce and Richard Neufeld).

$$\bullet \quad \bullet \quad \bullet \quad \bullet \quad \bullet$$

Tipsiness, a forgivable offence in the dancing dildo affair, has always played a role in night sittings, whether or not they are preceded by a formal dinner break. If not, some members are expected to do a first shift in debate after grabbing a bite to eat in the few minutes before the House resumes. Before the second or a later shift, a proper meal in the legislative dining room, with a glass or three of wine for some members, becomes a more and more desperately needed refuelling the longer the night debate goes on. Premier Bill Bennett—no teetotaler, unlike his father—instituted morning sittings in an effort to reduce if not eliminate night sittings and the incidence of inebriated debate. His move was prompted in part by one of the Social Credit Klan—Kerster of Kahl, Kempf and Kerster, who unseated NDP Premier Dave Barrett in the 1975 election—unseating himself one night when he leaned back too far in his chair and noisily fell out of it. It was generally assumed that he was taking a nap after a few drinks in the dining room, or elsewhere. He may have simply been bored to snore by the debate. Answering objections that morning sittings instead of evening ones meant less access for workingmen and -women, Bennett said more of the people's business would get done in the morning because "members don't put Scotch on their cornflakes."

The standing order urging temperance in debate refers, in part, to moderation not abstinence. Imbibing alcoholic beverages tends to instill a measure of non-partisan *bonhomie*, and may be excused on the grounds that the hyper-ventilation of hyper-partisan debate is very stressful and justifies indulgence in and of rowdy irrelevance as a side effect of lessened tension. That doesn't mean it goes unpunished. Struggling for *gravitas* like a drunk for an appearance of sobriety, Socred Speaker Ed Smith once admonished members for "hurling epitaphs" at one another.

Non-partisan camaraderie may develop among MLAs when a committee goes on the road or they share a floatplane, dinner and drinks, and a room (if not a bed) for the night in some remote coastal village. Committees sent out to take the pulse of the province on some issue(s) can generate a lot of interest. Audiences include people who have stored up anti-government feelings (specific and general), as well as more idiosyncratic ones, that they have to get off their chest. Off-the-top and off-the-wall presentations are in part the result of an informal, come-one-come-all atmosphere that is (to some degree deliberately) encouraged. Pre-registration does not prevent garrulous cranks and other trouble-makers getting in. Any attempt to exclude them would provoke charges of anti-democratic elitism, garnering adverse publicity, as would strict enforcement of House rules on irrelevance and repetition. Unless there are severe time constraints—an appointment with the people at the next stop, say—it's customary, after the more or less formal part of the meeting is over, to have an open-mic Q&A session, another opportunity to go far off topic.

— CHAPTER 12 —

Responsive Government
and Comparative Irresponsibility

Canada's parliamentary systems, federal and provincial, make committees of the legislature powerless compared to those of the separately powerful U.S. Congress. At the start of every legislative session in B.C. a list of committees is announced, with members selected by caucus and on the basis of party seat numbers in the House. The government decides which "standing" committees will be activated. Apart from a few traditional regulars, committees play a minor role in a session; but "special" ones launched in response to media and other public pressure for action on a long-neglected or newly eruptive problem may continue to sit and work between sessions. Many political commentators have decried the subservience of committees to the will and whim of the executive council (or Privy Council in Ottawa). It is all part of what makes for what Francis Fukuyama calls "state capacity," a mixed blessing of parliamentary systems of government. The freedom of action enjoyed by U.S. congressional committee chairpersons is cause for Canadian awe and envy. A Commons finance committee's interrogation of the WE charity's executives and of Liberal government ministers, including the PM, was hampered less by (the now universal) Covid distancing protocols and remote telecommunication glitches than by the committee Chair threatening to suspend proceedings whenever Conservative MP Pierre Poilièvre wouldn't stop talking after his allotted time had expired.

The American separation of powers gives executive power (the administration of government) to the President and his unrestricted choice of cabinet officers; and he has his own, singular national mandate. Congress's mandate is national too, but fractured and factional—by House and Senate and by political party. If the President's party has a majority in House and Senate, there is unitary government—balanced by appeal to the third co-equal branch, the Supreme Court (which, along with many lower courts, now has a 6-3 majority of conservative justices appointed by the political wiles of GOP Senate Majority Leader Mitch McConnell). One-party rule is checked by two-year turnover in the House and six-year security of tenure in the Senate, insofar as that means some Senators may outlast some Presidents.

The U.K. (Westminster model) parliamentary system keeps the democratic beast somewhat at bay by indirect election of the state's political leader. Unlike the U.S. President, with a separate democratic mandate, the Prime Minister can be voted directly into that office only by the caucus, or by a convention or polling of the membership, of a party that has a majority of seats in and/or the confidence of the House of Commons. (Whether the U.K.'s Conservative Party government and its DUP ally had that confidence while its Brexit sheaves were scythed down by members of its own and other parties is moot, if only because the official opposition Labour Party would not move a motion of non-confidence.) The leader of a party that has the next-biggest number of seats is potentially the next Prime Minister, or Premier of an Australian state or Canadian province. However, they can be made, or feel compelled, to resign after party heavyweights (including the leader, even one who is an incumbent PM or Premier) have read the writing on the subway walls. The general electorate is not formally consulted about the resignation of a Prime Minister or Premier—but a general election may, as elsewhere, be about a PM's or Premier's performance. Unlike American impeachment trials, the removal of a PM or Premier is a process neither captivating nor lengthy. Then there is the unique Australian leadership "spill." On 14 September 2015, some unhappy Liberal (governing) Party caucus members got together with some others and discovered a majority of them had had enough of their leader and voted him out, replacing PM Tony Abbott with former PM Malcolm Turnbull. Party soundings and public opinion polling had no doubt occurred. But Australians woke up to discover that "their" Prime Minister had been ousted by a caucus coup. The same thing then happened to Turnbull.

It has been said that the Westminster unitary model, uniting legislative with executive-administrative power, vests "decisive power over the legislature in the prime minister and his cabinet." The Australian example belies that power, which is limited in general practice by the susceptibility and unpredictability of legislatures in session assembled. The Brexit parliamentary shambles was predictable because of the existential nature of the issue. But all those MPs gave a much better picture of the collective British mind than did the Leave and Remain campaigns—the other third of public opinion was of several intermediate shades, and the House that then Prime Minister Theresa May built reflected that fact. Boris Johnson's trouncing of Labour with a 2% popular-vote swing in the 2019 general election is a comment on both the first-past-the-post electoral system and Jeremy Corbyn's decision to campaign with a platform from 1945. PM Johnson seems to think he can keep his troops loyal for the years, not months, that Euro-negotiations will take to arrive at a less than desirable but tolerable arrangement. He may avail himself of the heavy and hoary three-line whip, or not, and either way eat the democratic pudding. In theory, representative government is made stronger by being more representative; but the ever-popular (and usually fragile) united front requires compromise with annoying dissenters. And the old fairground game never ends: PM Punch has to keep a stick ready to swing at one or more pop-up caucus Judys.

In pre-Confederation days, there was a lot of so-called responsible government in the Canadian colonies. It was led by United Empire Loyalist "family compacts," and promulgated as an antidote to irresponsible representative democracy, in particular the raucous and rapacious kind practised in the breakaway United States. Canada has had its own version of federated representative democracy for quite some time now. However, the idea of responsible government that listens and responds to people's demands and complaints, but does not encourage the people's involvement in their elected (or appointed) representatives' deliberations, has deep roots in Canada's political imagination. From time to time Canadians wonder if we should not have some of the following: all sorts of legislative committees using constitutionally separate powers to publicly consult and energetically interrogate all sorts of people—and other manifestations of popular participation in American government. But the men who "framed" the U.S. constitution left a lot of reconstruction to be done, and deliberately divided the powers bestowed by democratic election in order to deflect and divert mass movements of opinion. In addition, they bequeathed what many Americans now regard as an anachronistic and thoroughly discredited device: the Electoral College, designed to thwart the political will of a national majority.

· · · · ·

In response to a far from mass movement, the first Campbell Liberal government decided to do something about the dog-eared file on proportional representation (PR). So it created a novelty (for the rest of Canada as well as B.C.), the Citizens' Assembly on Electoral Reform, charged with choosing an alternative to the existing first-past-the-post (FPTP) electoral system or staying with it. Other provinces followed suit, starting with Ontario. Justin Trudeau campaigned on a promise that the 2015 election would be the last federal one with FPTP. As PM, he put a political novice in charge of the PR file; she seems to have been told to dog it. PR is an idea at least as old as J.S. Mill's *Representative Government*. During WWI, a U.K. Speaker's Conference recommended the single transferrable vote (STV) ballot for some constituencies and the alternative vote (AV) ballot for some others. Neither was adopted. AV was used (or rather, abused) in B.C. in 1952. Minor-party votes were transferred in order to push a front-running candidate over the threshold, not to achieve PR. As soon as Premier Bennett got a Social Credit Party majority of seats, his government legislated AV's replacement by "good old" FPTP.

In 2004, B.C.'s new citizens' assembly recommended STV, which was placed before the B.C. electorate in a referendum. Other than the two aboriginals, members of this assembly were selected on a gender-balanced basis, by each of B.C.'s then 79 ridings choosing two from a list of constituents who had expressed an interest in serving. They were "ordinary" voters with no special background in electoral studies; but it's safe to assume that most of them put themselves on the list out of some dissatisfaction with the current voting system. The assembly opted for a form of STV used in two national states, Eire and Malta, and in one Australian state, Tasmania. (For what it's worth, Tasmania is home to the Tasmanian devil, a "flesh-eating marsupial of aggressive disposition"; Malta has become one of the most corrupt countries in Europe; and at a public meeting in B.C., a visiting Irish political scientist delivered a spirited attack on STV.) Under the chosen STV option, voters may select, *in order of their preference*, two or more candidates on their (single) constituency ballot. If one candidate is chosen first by a simple majority of voters, an outright winner can be declared. His/her surplus first-place votes are added to the next-most-preferred candidate's count (and, if necessary, second-choice votes) until there is a second "winner"—and so on down the list until second, third and other choices can no longer be combined to get another candidate over the constituency threshold. PR advocates say it "wastes" fewer votes, thus re-enfranchising many of the majority of voters in most elections under the current system.

STV is easy for voters—and a boon for those who dislike a stark choice or feel they have been cornered into plumping. However, as described by the Irish government's website on the subject, vote counters use a formula to assign voters' choices for second (place), third (show) and others that is a veritable Black Box of Blarney, transferring votes in a way that's more about number-crunching than voter preference. There were warnings of voter confusion about the STV option and, if it were implemented, governmental gridlock or instability. Another conservative ally, voter inertia, failed to materialize. The turnout for the referendum asking voters to say yes or no to STV was relatively high (61%); and it was chosen by almost 60% of them; but referendum rules required a no-less-than-60% vote for approval. The dragon of greater democratic choice was defeated by what some might call a technicality—on the grounds that a bar of anything more than 50%+1 is somewhat arbitrary. Why 60%? Why not 55, or 65, or 95 (a majority regularly "achieved" by some regimes)? In a 2009 follow-up referendum that asked B.C. voters to choose between FPTP and STV, it lost (40% in favour). Turnout was 55% for that question, which had been added to a general election ballot.

• • • • •

The shock of collision between the reality of indirect, representative, party-based democracy and a fervent belief in direct, grass-roots democracy was evident in Canada's "coalition crisis" of 2008-'09—which turned into the "prorogation crisis." Stephen Harper's minority Conservative government confronted an agreement among the leaders of the three other parties to vote as one against certain measures being proposed by the government. One that was a matter of (budget money) supply would be seen to call for a vote of confidence in the government, and its defeat to mean dissolution and a general election soon after the last one. (Harper had a bigger share of the popular vote and of seats in the House of Commons than before, but he was still in a minority.) Objections were rife about the legitimacy of an insiders' political manoeuvre. The initial reaction was one of incredulity that the rudderless Liberals, the socialist NDP and the separatist Bloc Québécois could agree and coalesce on anything. This reaction was helped by two things: (1) Liberal leader Stéphane Dion had resigned after his party's defeat and then returned as interim leader for coalition talks; (2) he and the NDP's Jack Layton could be running a coalition government without Bloc participation but dependent on their votes—and they had made it clear that they would vote against whatever they didn't like. (Liberal heir-presumptive Michael Ignatieff prudently did not get involved; and later led his party to one of its worst defeats by the Conservatives.) Some people derived some satisfaction from the prospect of victory for the overall popular-vote majority. Conservatives went ballistic because they thought their vote would be "stolen" if the election result were overturned by a cabal of parties representing electoral minorities who had neither singly nor collectively endorsed the plot. All protest and premature elation were checked—not silenced—by the constitutional fact that the fulcrum of political power is the House of elected representatives, where party-seat numbers mean more than popular-vote numbers. Even with a PR voting system, a party with a plurality of seats, regardless of their constituency distribution, can form government—depending, of course, on what minority members decide to do.

Rather than expose the embryonic coalition to the test of a House vote—not to mention his party to a possible election so soon after the last one—the PM had recourse to a questionable constitutional gambit. He asked the Governor-General for prorogation of the barely-begun session, a move widely criticized as an anti-democratic appeal to the royal prerogative. The government (1) knew that all party coffers were seriously depleted, and no one truly wanted another general election; and (2) calculated that a respite from parliamentary debate would deprive both the incubating coalition and the hyperventilated constitutional crisis of much-needed oxygen. And so it proved. The government and the system survived until two years later the system produced a Conservative popular vote of a sliver under 40% that gave them a majority of House seats. It wasn't long before cries erupted from across the opposition spectrum that the government was using its majority to ram through measures—for which it had no proper mandate, given its popular-vote deficit—that were going to destroy parliamentary democracy, the nation and the biosphere.

Despite a show of consultation, a sitting PM or Premier has the power to "persuade" the head of state to do the government's bidding and not seriously contemplate seeking alternative counsel. They are rarely denied. Two who were are Prime Minister Mackenzie King of Canada in the 1926 King-Byng affair and Prime Minister Gough Whitlam of Australia in the 1974 Whitlam-Kerr affair. These "affairs" were crises because in both cases the Governor-General (G-G) denied the PM dissolution and an election and called on the Leader of the Opposition to form a government. In the Canadian case, King asked for a second dissolution nine months after the first one, which had led to a coalition government; and the G-G rejected another election. King quickly bounced back in a snap election called by his successor. Whitlam never returned. King exploited "imperial interference" (which helped him in Quebec), then led the push for the 1931 Statute of Westminster, which recognized the reality of a "Commonwealth of [sovereign] Nations"—i.e., the old white dominions and (nominally) the new Irish Free State—under the British Crown.

Faced with an NDP-Green alliance, after she won the 2017 election with 43 seats to the NDP's 41 and the Green Party's 3, B.C. Premier Christy Clark put a throne speech before the new parliament and was, in effect, laughed out of the House. Her defeat—closely followed by her resignation as party leader and MLA—was caused by her having composed a throne speech (government agenda) that rewrote the recent Liberal Party election platform in what looked like a cynical attempt to lure Green MLA votes. The Lieutenant-Governor (L-G) was not amused by Clark's request for dissolution and a general election two months after the last one. So she invited the NDP to try to form a government, which they did under Premier John Horgan, with Green Party support. One Liberal MLA agreed to defect, in effect, and break a tie vote by becoming Speaker. The deal held for three years. Horgan broke an agreement with former Green Party leader Andrew Weaver by calling an early provincial election, which gave him a government majority.

The U.K. head of state—who performs the same function for Australia, Canada and New Zealand—is "consulted" by her council of state in the person of the Prime Minister. The monarch may "advise" him or her. But these chats are "privy" (as in the seemingly inescapable association of politics and government with lavatories), and need have no effect on governmental action. If they improbably did, nobody would know. If pressed, the PM could simply say that the monarch was very but non-specifically supportive of good government. Such meetings are a matter of courtesy, and paying homage to the head of state is not just for kings and queens.

Canada's Governor-Generals have been distinguished Canadian citizens since 1952. Before that, they were superannuated British peers of the realm. They have always been seen as above, or past caring about, the political fray. None of them has the celebrity heft of the monarch they represent. Perhaps operating on the premise that any publicity is good for a public office, G-G Julie Payette has been making expensive demands of her vice-regal budget and staff and allegedly encouraging an "abusive" workplace. G-Gs come and go, after doing the ribbon-cutting duties required by their job description, and showing the flag at home and abroad as "requested" by Prime Ministers. The current G-G looks like one that might go before her time is up—which might be a sort of scandal that tarnishes the image of not just her office but of constitutional monarchy itself, as practiced in Canada at least. Australia has always been more anti-monarchist (and anti-Limey) than Canada, in spite of the francophone Quebec factor.

PMs seem to lord it over their head of state—they know that the G-G is a kind of billboard in the eyes of most Canadians; and a PM's family has acquired some of the royal one's celebrity, a shared diminution of dignity. This is accentuated when the official residence(s) or business tower(s) of a head of state, or President or Prime Minister, are (partly or occasionally) occupied by their adult children, whose doings can do great damage to the parent's public image—as has occurred with children of both Queen Elizabeth and King Donald—and turn the "royal house" into a sit-com.

Premiers and Prime Ministers call upon the stand-in for the head of state when they want something that requires his or her imprimatur: swearing in of a new cabinet, dissolution, or royal assent to legislative bills. B.C.'s L-G has been ordered out of bed in the middle of the night and hauled slipper-shod into the legislative chamber to sit on his throne in pyjamas and dressing-gown, there to say and do nothing as the list of a session's bills and the assent formula are read out for His Honour as if he were not there. Although this dumb show is constitutionally obligatory, at this stage a bill has been read a third time, and "it is an act"—except that a statute often includes proclamation dates attached to all or parts of it, when it or they will actually come into effect. The rigmarole of royal assent seems to somehow dim the L-G's lustre. Is that the price of House convenience—because members want to wrap up a session and get home, to a bar, on a plane for a vacation, or just show him or her who's boss?

— CHAPTER 12 (b) —

Like their American cousins, Canadian voters don't entirely trust their legislators and legislative systems. One common cause is the national capital's cultural as well as geographical remoteness from many of the nation's inhabitants—which affects Canada's rural and remote voters in provincial elections, too, although less so in the older and smaller Atlantic provinces. Another is the conviction that politicians can't help helping themselves, and their own or importunate constituents' pet projects, to extravagant amounts of taxpayers' money. There is also a long-held belief that once a politician is sent "abroad" to Ottawa or Washington, D.C., he never comes back home to find out what his constituents want but, rather, to tell them what they need and what their government wants. This belief is reinforced by a supplementary suspicion that both ordinary and cabinet members are too easily co-opted by long-serving personnel in the permanent civil service; or that they have corrupted it by appointing friends, family and partisans to public office.

Other than deadlock between their separate executive and legislative branches, and liberal-progressive bias in federal institutions and among national opinion-makers, American popular anger is directed at the degree of political influence wielded by special interests and their money—defence contractors, pharmaceutical companies, trial lawyers, etc., etc. Canada's more restrictive campaign finance laws somewhat reduce that influence in our elections and government. Members of Congress are in many cases hostages to a primary nomination process in which they have to compete for the support of wealthy donors (and their agendas). This dependence is more applicable to Representatives than Senators because of the formers' two-year term. Members of the House try to reduce their reliance on corporate and other "dark" money by gerrymandering their electoral districts, aided in doing that by state legislatures where their party is in the majority — a majority (invariably the national minority party) now seeking to change election rules in a way that would impair voter access to polling places and the ballot itself.

Canada has its own peculiar lightning rod for citizen anger over governmental irresponsibility and legislature chicanery. Our second (upper) chamber contains more than 100 richly remunerated Senators appointed—not elected—to represent various regions and minorities in a country physically larger but with about one-tenth the population of the U.S. There is an *idée fixe* that the Senate is beyond reform because the Quebec contingent represents not only the province's population but also one of Canadian Confederation's founding peoples. Quebec is the heartland of Canada's French fact. It is also a world *francophonie* leader for scattered Franco-American facts: Acadian francophones in New Brunswick and the other Atlantic provinces (and in Maine?); groups of varying francophone vitality in Ontario, Manitoba and elsewhere in western Canada; and the French history of North America as a whole. The Senate's delaying function, the hackneyed "sober second look," is of brief duration and, in spite of some distinguished non-partisan appointees, vitiated by its history as a sinecure for party faithful of the government in power. Long Liberal dominance in the House of

Commons, interspersed by Conservative governments inflating their Senate numbers by "packing," aided by death and other attrition, did little to support the Senate's claim to be a place for less partisan deliberation. News from the "Red Chamber" has featured debate by kazoo, staged fisticuffs and exorbitant expense claims that lax (unenforced or unenforceable) Senate rules encourage. Abolitionist public opinion, which subsides as each "new" Senate scandal does, trends ever upward. Senate reports, some expertly written, continue to be filed and forgotten (except by a few academics). It is no disparagement of individual Senate luminaries to say that this expensive excrescence on the legislative anatomy has a corrosive effect on confidence in and respect for all federal political institutions.

The ongoing scandal of Canada's Senate was renewed in May 2013. Senator Mike Duffy—this episode was named after him, but other senatorial shoes kept dropping—accepted a personal cheque for $90,000 from Prime Minister Harper's chief of staff with which to repay what he (Duffy) owed the Senate for improper use of public funds on his travel, housing and other personal living expenses. His benefactor had a Bay Street (Canada's minor-league version of Wall Street) background, which could perhaps excuse any lack of familiarity with public service rules—if not the PM for appointing him. Duffy's background as a former member of the Ottawa press gallery should have taught him that to accept Nigel Wright's gift would place him in an untenable position. Whether or not he was simply buried by bookkeeping and made an accounting error, it is well established that public servants do not accept personal gifts from Jane Q. Public, let alone from someone in a position of power and influence. The perception of a compromising obligation can be enough to compel resignation.

Duffy has asserted that the method of repaying the money he owed was approved or at least condoned by the PMO. The PM's response was to throw both Duffy and Wright under the bus. The Senate was urged to do something it had apparently never done before: undertake an investigation of the "affair" by a Senate special committee and a full audit of all Senators. Duffy and two other big spenders were expelled from the Conservative caucus, then suspended without pay. A Prime Minister telling the Senate to show its independence by doing what he thought it should do raised some awkward questions. The 800-pound answer to all of them is that the PM appoints Senators and the Senate is an annex of the PMO. Justin Trudeau, recently elected Liberal Party leader, responded to the exposure of at least one delinquent Liberal Senator by expelling them all from caucus and claiming they were now Independents. Whether or not that freed them from the taint of Senate misconduct, they are now (theoretically) free from caucus discipline and able to delay or otherwise impede a Liberal government's order of business.

Prime Minister Harper got a quick unanimous no from the Supreme Court in answer to his quick and calculated request for a ruling on whether the Senate can be altered without agreement of all the provinces. Constitutional pundits say the Senate cannot be abolished without a constitutional conference that no one really wants and is an abhorrent prospect for many. One Canadian academic said that the experience of both the Meech Lake and the Charlottetown accord failing "drove Canada to the brink of extinction." (A successful result was appointments to the Senate and Supreme Court henceforth requiring consultation with the provinces.) Another such first ministers' conference could not be confined to Senate reform or abolition—a Pandora's box of constitutional complaints would be opened. An NDP Leader of the Opposition's statement that the Senate has never done anything of value is not true. But it challenges the "other place" to defend itself and its plush appurtenances. Tom Mulcair's promise that if he became Prime Minister (which seemed quite possible at one point), he would put Senate abolition to a national yes-or-no vote (as Eire did), forced those with a vested interest in Senate preservation to think seriously about its reform—until his party came third in the 2015 federal election.

Although at the time it seemed a knee-jerk reaction to PM Harper's peremptory way of dealing with Senate misconduct, Trudeau's "liberation" of Liberal Senators may turn out to be a fruitful initiative. If enough Liberal Senators were to take on their new independence as a serious public service remit and if that were to cause enough friction in government to arouse public interest, the weight of public opinion might shift in favour of major Senate reform. Or it might create a final impasse that leads to abolition—and Quebec settling for a unicameral, multi-party Parliament in which its "block" of MPs would have a veto over anything that would derogate from its existing freedom of action as a nation within a nation. In other words, we would "keep buggering on" as before, but without an expensive supernumerary institution.

Canada's Senate is three-U: unelected, and therefore unaccountable (directly to the citizenry), and unknown (to the same citizenry). As a side benefit of the Duffy affair, the public was afforded a rare peek at what exactly it is paying for (Wright's $90,000 notwithstanding). Most residents of provinces or regions that Senators supposedly represent only learn of their activities (even of their very existence) when scandal erupts. An imperishable image left from the Duffy affair is a very proper lady Senator saying, in answer to a reporter's inquiry: "Do you know what we have to put up with? Air Canada serves its Camembert cold!" (To spare the Senator's feelings, this story may be partly apocryphal, and should be hedged, like so many others, with the following comment by a very shrewd historian: "All too often invented dialogues and vivid incidents found in 'primary sources' do not describe what actually happened but have a convenient explanatory function.") Regardless of its comedy, her comment did nothing to quell public rage, needless to say.

Senate appointments are announced without fanfare, almost as if a bit shameful—which, unless an appointee is a well-known high achiever in business, sport, science or the arts (including entertainment and media, mixed or not), is how they're frequently viewed.

The structural framework of some states has been bent, even broken, by political forces it could no longer contain. How many Canadians— and which ones where—feel that "their" Senate is an existential issue for Canada? Could there be a U.S.-style conference of both Houses that confines itself to a new division of their respective powers? If the Senate were given more power, and thereby more responsibility, would Senators act less like aging adolescents and premature pensioners? Could the provinces agree on a Senate election system that keeps Quebec's "special place" in Confederation, and again postpone debate of rep-by-pop versus equality for provinces (not to mention special provision for aboriginal representation)? If new arrangements were agreed upon, could they be selectively enacted using the 7+50 rule (seven provinces and at least 50% of the population agreeing)? Would any government of a province whose legislature rejected a Senate reform package be obliged to put it—and possible secession from Canada—to a referendum?

— CHAPTER 13 —

Same Mother, Different Father

The USMCA (the new, improved NAFTA) is still, *pace* President Trump (peace be upon him, prays Nancy Pelosi), a North American house with a semi-detached basement, Mexico. The basement is crowded with Amerindian refugees, mostly from Guatemala and Honduras, where a deepening ecological crisis, assisted by large-landowner regimes in league with drug cartels, has forced *campesinos* off their subsistence farms and into extreme poverty; activist opponents of regime policies are murdered. The Trump administration has muscled Mexico into being a holding pen for these refugees and asylum-seekers. Canada need not worry over-much about re-export of the indigent indigenous who wriggled in under or over Trump's barriers—once again, we're saved by a cold climate; except that some experts say climate change could open up lands north of 60° latitude to agriculture. (It should be noted that Latin-American agricultural labourers in Ontario's Windsor-Essex fields, working south of Detroit, have not been treated well by that province's regulations.)

The Mexican basement is a boiler room generating dynamic energy bursts for the American economic engine—and eager recruits into U.S.

military and paramilitary employment (not just Latino police chiefs but also members of the U.S.-Mexico border patrol). In the eyes of ICE and other U.S. gatekeepers, Mexico is seen as a conduit for alien hordes. Then there's the myth of American job loss, for people who have repeatedly proven unwilling to do the work on offer. (A northern U.S. dairy farmer found that the only person who would work the long hours of barn-cleaning and milking, including in winter conditions, was an immigrant from Mexico.)

The most livable rooms in the NAFTA (I or II) house are in the mostly temperate latitudes of the U.S. In this part of the house there are many mansions: "great" living-rooms, dining (banquet) rooms, enormous kitchens and bathrooms, dens and (open-plan, open-door) bedrooms. To get into them, occupants of the basement must climb a long, dangerous staircase; their safe arrival is a gamble, and their stay not assured. In the attic are a lot of Canadian maiden aunts peering down through a trap door in a mixture of trepidation and titillation. The trap door is also an escape hatch, through which bored Canadians just drop in— and stay if they want to. All are consumed by the American spectacle. Some react with Milton's "Licence they mean when they cry liberty." Others exclaim: "We want some of that." Note the "some." (In his history of the 1812-'15 war, Alan Taylor has an intriguing description, based on contemporaneous diaries and other documents, of "late Loyalist" emigrants from the still new republic travelling north to restart their lives in British North America and then deciding they were better off where they had come from; some did the reverse, some a double reverse. This was occurring in the middle of a shooting war.)

Few Americans (and not many Canadians) understand exactly how it happened when the Canadian economy was crippled by a transcontinental railways blockade, an initiative of tribal leaders (mostly those pesky Mohawks) in sympathy with Wet'suwet'en chiefs' opposition to a pipeline being built through their territory in northwestern B.C. Rather than discuss the legalities or conflicting rights involved, I would like to say something about the historical arc of this dispute in the Canadian attic of North America. Attics are places for storage of memories, usually in the shape of memorabilia. In the attic of the mind dwells the id, which has nothing do with sex acts, only with the sex drive. And that is about imagined sex, and the memory of good sex and not so good sex—about anticipation, anxiety and regret. One could say that there's a lot of reflection, and contemplation, going on in the id as well as in the ego and superego. Out of the grave of their expectations frustrated, denied, repressed and suppressed, the spirits of their ancestors arose and drove the hereditary chiefs to make one more last stand for their ancient connection to their land, which they have traditionally conceived of in spiritual terms—even more so now that the industrialized global economy has taken physical occupation of it.

Many environmentalists who support the hereditary chiefs and the stand they've taken seem to think that their traditional territory—the one they once roamed over, leaving a light footprint—should be preserved. But as what? They can't return to pre-contact days for many reasons, not the least of which is the way their lives have changed, willy-nilly, since contact. The outcome of stopping "progress" could be a park reserve in which they re-enact parts in a "natural history" play for tourists. It's safe to say that many tribal members, both young and not so young, would resist that outcome—and not primarily for spiritual reasons. (Some aboriginal leaders, such as Haisla chief Ellis Ross, express skepticism about native Indian spirituality: "We murdered, and we pillaged and we took slaves. People talk about…you have to pray to the Great Spirit. There was no great spirit in Haisla history.")

In both countries the proportion of aboriginals (including those of mixed parentage, or Métis, as their status is now recognized and named in Canada) is very low: 1.6% in the U.S. and roughly 2.5% in Canada, of whom more than half are Métis. As outlined earlier, the history of non-aboriginal settlement in Canada was always threatening for aboriginals but not overwhelming until the 20th century. There are many places in Canada, especially in the north, where aboriginals live, on or off reserve, with only intermittent contact with non-aboriginals. Wet-'suwet'en territory was a bit like that until a road to supply pipeline construction materials began to be pushed through, and the arrival of a more regular RCMP presence. Which is not to say that the native people there were still living in tepees and on food they hunted and gathered. Another disturbing factor was native involvement in honky(-tonk) commerce and industry. Quite a few local aboriginals got construction jobs, working with white folk and meeting with them on work-related issues, not just socially. The conflict was not about some Quebeckers wanting to clear more Indian land so they could play more golf—but Kanesatake Mohawks saw an affinity between that and what was happening over 2,000 klicks away from them.

People impatient with aboriginal cultural-spiritual resistance to development of various kinds (of whom I confess to be one from time to time) need to remember their own anger when some blankety-blank developer has cut down a grove of trees they had long enjoyed aesthetically as well as recreationally. How long have you and yours felt the presence of that grove—even in what you may think is a spiritually uplifting way? The intersection of Indian land claims and the eco-climatological crisis has made not only the oil and gas industry nervous. Justin "Reconciliation" Trudeau's Minister of Crown—Indigenous Relations Carolyn Bennett and her B.C. counterpart Scott Fraser seem to have persuaded the Wet'suwet'ens to negotiate some kind of better deal for themselves—enough that their Mohawk allies abandoned their railfreight blockade. Three days of talks produced an agreement to later have more talks—not about the pipeline but about Wet'suwet'en land title claims. Meanwhile Coastal GasLink, the company building the pipeline, wants permission for some pre-build surveying, which will be protested, blockaded and then protected by another provocative RCMP presence. This stasis needs a conciliatory contribution (royalty payments?) from NDP B.C. Premier John Horgan, who thought he had a deal with the elected tribal council.

·　·　·　·　·

Notwithstanding its long-lived social-democratic party, the CCF-NDP—a lot of whose supporters would be anxious if it somehow took power in Ottawa—Canada is a conservative country. There's not much difference between the national Liberals and the national Conservatives. The centre shifted to the right when the latter jettisoned the so-called Red Tories (but most provincial Tories still call themselves the Progressive-Conservative Party). Both parties rely on hefty contributions from (and are thereby in some way indebted to) large Canadian private-sector corporations. Canadians generally prefer that Grits and Tories remain as similar in outlook as they can contrive to be while giving the electorate a real choice on subsets of policies (e.g., pollution cap-and-trade versus a carbon tax). The American political scene has helped bring about an increase in Canadian bush-league dirty politics. The following is a recent example: broadcasting a speech against same-sex marriage by Conservative leader Andrew Scheer when he was a new MP in 2005 was countered by pictures of Liberal PM Justin Trudeau in blackface when he was a schoolteacher in Vancouver. Responses were a statement from Scheer accepting general Canadian acceptance of same-sex marriage, but no endorsement of laws to that effect; and a Trudeau apology for youthful indiscretion, but no comment on teachers setting an example.

Immigration is, as it has been in the U.S. for many years, an issue bedevilled by latent racism and xenophobia. A former Conservative MP,

Maxime Bernier, who failed in his bid to become leader of the party, started his own, the People's Party, whose main platform plank was fewer immigrants—"was" says what happened to the party in the 2019 election. The face of the Liberal Party of Canada is strikingly multiracial (or they deliberately put that face forward on TV); and the leader of the NDP is a turbaned Sikh—"turbaned" because an NDP Premier of B.C., Ujjal Dosanjh, was a Sikh who did not wear a turban. Unlike Jagmeet Singh, he (but for the fact that he became a Liberal) might have retained more NDP seats in Quebec, where wearing religious insignia when working for the public is now illegal. Bernier is Québécois, and as such no friend of immigration that would, as it were, deracinate French Canada (and perhaps, also in his view, the rest of Canada). Bernier and the current Premier of Quebec, François Legault, are coy secularists, trailing their alluring (and confusing) secular slip. As did Stephen Harper, a "covert evangelical" Christian and fervent friend of Israel—which most evangelicals tend to be; and part of that is willingness to join U.S. "crusades" against Israel's Muslim enemies (e.g., in the Afghanistan quagmire), as distinct from Jean Chrétien's non-committal "thanks, but no thanks" reply to George W. Bush's invitation to join his "coalition of the willing" invasion of Iraq. Bernier professes to be a libertarian—somewhat along the lines of his old boss in cabinet, PM Harper, who told the world in an election victory speech, directed straight at his back bench, that his government would not support any legislative bills any of them might introduce on the settled issues of abortion and same-sex marriage. Legault seems open for ideological business, demonstrating his "fair and balanced" implementation of his contentious ban on religious apparel by having the crucifix over the Speaker's chair in the National Assembly quietly removed. Both Scheer and Trudeau are Roman Catholics, the former seemingly more devout than the latter, who returned to the fold (it is said) after the death of his brother Michel. Conclusion: unlike in America, very little political benefit is derived in Canada from making a show of your religious belief, or unbelief, nor (so far) from being openly anti-immigrant. The Conservative Party's electoral problem is its harbouring a stubbornly intolerant faction of so-called social conservatives.

In one of his "Sunshine Sketches" Stephen Leacock (called Canada's Mark Twain by some) describes a small-town Ontario political campaign meeting in the 1920s. The audience reaction is likened to the flat, unblinking gaze of fish eyes. Some may have been asleep, the men being mostly farmers who worked in their fields all day while their wives were at home cooking, cleaning and mending; and this was a rare opportunity to get out and relax—they didn't much care if they weren't entertained. Their folded arms, silent hands, expressionless faces and sub-susurrus breathing made for an unbreachable barrier against anything the speaker could dream up and promise them. They may have been leery of any political rhetoric, having heard or read the sort employed leading up to a fairly recent and unusual wartime election called by Unionist (Conservative) Prime Minister Robert Borden. It was dangerously and predictably divisive, because of French- and "British"-Canadian differences over the need for military conscription. Former Liberal PM and acknowledged leader of francophone opinion Wilfrid Laurier warned that "appeals to passion are always sure to bring forth a crop of prejudice." Which is exactly what happened in 1917-'18, and lingered on long after.

Imperial trade preference and WWI imperial sentiment are now a distant memory. But some intimate "family" memories can remain active for a long time. The Quebec vehicle licence tag, *Je me souviens*, may or may not be a mystery to Americans as it flashes by on its way to Florida sunshine; but what is being remembered is the Battle of the Plains of Abraham in 1759, and the end of the French empire in North America (not fully finalized until Napoleon sold the Louisiana Territory to President Jefferson). It also marked the beginning of a fully Franco-*American* presence in North America. One American author, who went to school in Maine (the name, incidentally, of one of France's regions), has written that Lewiston is a French-Canadian city (see Amy Bass, *One Goal*). When the Quebec alliance of church and state resisted military conscription of *habitant* farmers and their sons in 1917-'18, it was fighting against an unholy triple alliance of Anglo-American perfidy and French apostasy. The second round of that struggle pitted a dwindling band of Catholic nationalists and friends of Catholic dictators like Franco and Salazar (with the tacit support of the Quebec church) against other Québécois who were willing to fight to defeat atheistic fascism even if it meant an alliance with atheistic communism.

The War Measures Act of 1914 was invoked in 1939, in force throughout WWII, and used to strip Japanese-Canadians of civil liberties and property rights and place them in concentration camps—as was done in the U.S. It was not used during the Korean War, and used for the third and final time in October 1970 during the FLQ (Front de libération du Québec) crisis. It was replaced with the Emergencies Act in 1988. Because the FLQ crisis was one of apprehended insurrection, and the prospect of civil war was being seriously considered, PM Pierre Trudeau decided to take drastic action and put the Canadian Army— and martial law—onto the streets of Montreal and Ottawa. People anywhere in Canada who were suspected of supporting separatism (even if they gave no material aid to separatists' bombing and kidnapping terrorism) could be rounded up and summarily jailed. Trudeau's actions were condemned as an abrogation of civil liberties, particularly freedom of speech, and the ancient law of habeas corpus. Two factors can be cited in his defence. First, Quebec Premier Robert Bourassa asked for heavy-duty federal help after the kidnapping of British consul James Cross and the kidnap and murder of Quebec Deputy Premier Pierre Laporte. Second, nobody was in a position to confidently assert that Trudeau was using "a sledgehammer to crack a nut" (the NDP leader's words). (No) thanks to the very unready yet all too willing RCMP, then new to the practice of counter-intelligence and counter-terrorism—this experience (or lack of it) prompted the creation of the Canadian Security Intelligence Service (CSIS, as in CIA)—no government knew anything reliable or actionable about FLQ structure, strategy and support. When a national security threat was perceived, the politician who 12 years later brought Canada its Charter of Rights and Freedoms seized the power available to him to act in what might be called the spirit of Hobbesian sovereignty. Also Hobbesian was his fearful appreciation, as another man of letters, of the political damage wrought by inflammatory rhetoric, as featured in a 1968 best-seller (in Quebec), *Les Nègres blanc d'Amérique* by Pierre Vallières (translated as *White Niggers of America*).

PM Justin Trudeau has been attacked for saying a few kind words about Fidel Castro when he died. It may have been in recognition of Fidel's willingness to take some FLQ ringleaders, who had hijacked a plane to Havana, off Trudeau *père*'s hands in the dénouement of the 1970 Quebec crisis. Imagine, just for the hell of it, Pierre on the phone to Fidel shortly after the plane took off: "Fidel, I have a favour to ask, as one who has lent moral support to your struggle against those silly U.S. sanctions. Could you look after some guys who murdered a Quebec cabinet minister?" Pause. Fidel: "Claro."

Canada has had a few larger-than-life political figures. Two obvious ones are John A. Macdonald and Louis Riel. The second was hanged for trying to remake the Canada of which the first was the prime mover. Riel is not diminished by being considered a bit of a madman—what his pupils thought of him in his self-exile to a Minnesota schoolroom, one can barely imagine; he returned to be hanged and become a martyr for aboriginal, Catholic and francophone rights (a self-image he held). Nor is Macdonald by being labelled a more or less functioning alcoholic. In a separate category, as the "father" of Canadian medicare, is Saskatchewan's first social-democratic Premier, Tommy Douglas. Like Sen. Harry Reid, Douglas was an amateur boxing champ—good preparation for his career as a Baptist preacher and left-wing politician.

Two of the strangest were Premier W.A.C. ("Wacky") Bennett of British Columbia and Prime Minister John ("Dief the Chief") Diefenbaker. Bennett had long electoral success—20 continuous years of Social Credit government (1952-72)—bashing the socialist CCF-NDP while using his government (and it was "his" government) to create public-sector corporations as a means of opening up the province to rapid industrial development. "The Chief" rode a wave of popular discontent, leading the Progressive-Conservatives to a 1957 upset of complacent federal Liberals, then a 1958 sweep, followed by his protracted decline into political impotence. But he kept the adulation of a dwindling band of faithful followers, as he stubbornly clung to the British Red Ensign while the new Canadian maple-leaf flag won ever more national support. When making his signature speech about his "vision of the north," his neck wattles would wobble as he climbed into full tremulous yet stentorian flight. He had been a (mostly criminal defence) lawyer, and passionate defender of civil rights, in a northerly Saskatchewan prairie town, Prince Albert, a riding he represented in Parliament for 40 years. He came late in life to and ill-prepared for the demands of running Canada's federal government. His party was a hopeful coalition of a not very progressive Progressive Party with one wanting more MPs to help it defeat the arrogant Liberals. His cabinet contained an ideological jumble, the kind that made life difficult for Mulroney's later (and last) P-C government. Dief's Minister of National Defence, Doug Harkness, was a hawk who argued vehemently for purchase of U.S. fighter jets, against supporters of Canada's home-grown Avro Arrow (which some aviation experts thought superior in every way). The External Affairs minister, Howard Green, was a believer in world government—a

Green before his time? The PM knew nothing of Quebec, let alone how to speak its language, and relied on cabinet colleague Pierre Sévigny to be his French lieutenant (a much-decorated WWII hero, he was acceptable to the Anglican party establishment). President Kennedy hated Diefenbaker, a reciprocal feeling.

To the above mix should be added Liberal leader, Diefenbaker punching-bag and Prime Minister (1963-'68), Lester Bowles ("Mike") Pearson, plus JFK's successor, Lyndon Baines Johnson. What brought this cast of characters together was the Columbia River Treaty, signed in early 1961 by Dief and Ike. It was spawned in part by the NAWAPA (not an Indian tribe but the North American Water and Power Alliance), a grandiose project dreamed up by the American Army Corps of Engineers in the 1950s. This Canadian-American concatenation has had an afterlife in the concept of Cascadia. It's the name for a vague community of interests among B.C. and (parts of) Alaska, Washington, Oregon and California, (some of) whose political, business and other leaders from time to time pay dreamy lip-service to it. The original idea was to divert flow from several rivers, chiefly the Columbia, through the Rocky Mountain Trench and thence mostly into the Colorado, life-blood of Arizona's and California's agro-industry—now an arterial trickle to Imperial Valley, where the desert used to bloom with 80% of North America's winter fruit and vegetables. NAWAPA was going to yield more benefits, especially in terms of water storage and hydroelectric power generation. It would have involved some 365 dams, ditches and devices (one for every day of each of the same number of years it would probably take to build, at a cost of many trillions in today's dollars.) Apart from the price tag, the whole idea met with furious protest over its damaging environmental, fisheries and other effects.

In the course of its 60–year history, the parties to the treaty have had to adjudicate complaints and disputes over energy/power distribution and various kinds of pollution. The treaty was the occasion for some well-wishing early in its life, in 1964, when Johnson and Pearson played away on B.C. Premier Bennett's home ground. The genial host dominated proceedings, having already driven a hard treaty bargain (according to American negotiators). The event was captured by *Vancouver Sun* cartoonist Len Norris: a top-down Cadillac (driven by B.C. Highways minister "Flying Phil" Gaglardi) speeding through Kootenay (spelled Kootenai in the U.S.) country, Bennett in the shotgun seat extolling the beauty and greatness of "his" province to Johnson, who looks like he has been trapped in the audience at an aliens' political convention, while wee Mikey Pearson, Prime Minister and Nobel peace prize winner, looks like an ignored infant trying to get the adults' attention.

• • • • •

In 1916 a young girl is travelling with her father, a widowed Manitoba quarryman who is moving to Indiana with a promise of work in its vast limestone deposits and a prospect of future wealth. She later recalls the trip: "As the miles clicked away, it seemed…the seriousness of the world was in retreat" (Carol Shields, *The Stone Diaries*). Her take on the blithe spirit of Americans' pursuit of happiness could be said to encapsulate what has driven generations of the "travellin' people" (Irish immigrants on their way through Canada to the U.S. in the 19th century), and does to this day for under- and unemployed men in Atlantic Canada: "I'm outta here, boy, goin' to the Boston States" (where, they need to believe, the streets are still paved with gold). Admittedly, until the slump in oil-patch jobs, they went west not south; but America is closer than Alberta—and they look and sound American, with the possible exception of Newfoundlanders (who are also unique among Canadians).

— CHAPTER 14 —

High Ways and Mean Streets

Machiavelli is best known as a psychologist of power relationships. The respect a political leader needs—and needs to earn—is much more than just fear of his power. Fearful followers or a fearful citizenry create a lot of extra work for a leader (or despot, as he would probably become very quickly if he didn't begin that way); and he would probably have to work harder and harder just to keep from feeling insecure himself. Having, or just feeling, the need to constantly fear-monger makes for a very fearful monger—a subject examined in Plato's dialogue *Gorgias*, where he talks about the unhappiness of tyrants. David Hume's insightful observation that wielding power successfully depends on some degree of willing acceptance from (at least a favoured) some of those on the receiving end—the "whom" in Lenin's terse saying about power, "Who, whom"—could be read as a gloss on Machiavelli's best-known work, *The Prince*. It's a treatise on the pathology of early modern Italian city-states and a DIY manual for surviving their politics, an aid to navigation of poorly charted waters and stormy seas. A captain of the ship of state has to sometimes rule with a rod of iron; nerves of well-tempered steel are also essential insofar as cultivation of and reliance on crew and passenger confidence are necessary. Simply bludgeoning people into submission is exhausting for everyone. If it's a ruler's only MO, he will end up ruling a hulk or a ghost ship—a result that has done nothing to deter some of the world's worst dictators. Two of Machiavelli's prescriptions for success in fluctuating political conditions are: (1) keep supporters and opponents wondering, a little off-balance, by alternating potlatch—an aspiring ruler needs wealth—and punishment; (2) play the lion convincingly because it increases the likelihood of not having to actually wreak merciless revenge.

The most important thing a ruler does is *far figura*—look good, cut a fine figure, make a confidence-inspiring impression, and have a commanding presence. Looking the part is as important as actually doing what it looks like one is doing. Even if his military record is glorious, a commander-in-chief should continue to be seen striding purposefully across the White House lawn to his waiting, fired-up Marine Corps helicopter. Some Presidents have been naturals at this role-playing or have had a long apprenticeship for the role (Reagan), some try too hard (Bush II), and some are, and look, self-conscious and uncomfortable, even shifty (Nixon). Trump just looked uncomfortably belligerent. Voters in modern democracies tend to want someone (male or female) whom they can imagine fronting with obvious conviction the enterprise of government—and to weed out people who, however worthy of high office, look…weedy. An obvious case is contrasting the armour-plated Margaret Thatcher and the dishevelled Michael Foot, a fine journalist and brave humanitarian who, in the 1983 U.K. election, led a fractured Labour Party to humiliating defeat against Conservative PM "Iron Lady" Thatcher (middle name Hilda, Old Norse for battle, as in the Falklands War).

As the old saying says, timing is everything. It is almost by definition that great success achieved by exceptional foresight followed promptly by breathtakingly effective action is reserved for a happy few. Most good timing is retrospective. The number of ideas and endeavours that failed because they were either premature or just too late is legion— although their originators may be celebrated posthumously. More important than timing (but closely connected), says another cliché, is luck. It is made by seizing success from a moment created by an acceleration of events and an unanticipated conjoining of factors known and unknown, some brought under control and others uncontrollable. Luck is *fortuna* in Machiavelli's language, and fortune favours the bold (not the brave). Another word for them is chancers—not compulsive gamblers but people willing to push at small openings. They don't trifle or flirt with Lady Fortune; they pursue her avidly, and court the danger of wearing out their welcome.

Machiavelli led a split life. At night he communed with the thoughts of Cicero, Livy and other illustrious shades of the ancient Roman republic, longing to live in his idealized version of their world. His day job was acting as a counsellor or adviser to Florence's republican government; and then, after its fall, seeking rehabilitation doing similar work for the new principality and its ruling family, by flattery of its head man Lorenzo de' Medici (the Magnificent). A lugubrious executive summary of *The Prince* would be along the following lines: "Good luck, Larry the Second. You're going to need it. Your regime is not hedged with divinity. Those days are gone. In spite of your secret machinations, you and your government are an open invitation to every adventurous malcontent wanting to take a chance on overthrowing you."

For politicians in a constitutional democracy, that seems a lesson both unnecessary and inappropriate (to speak in an appropriately anodyne New Age way). They can survive political death and lead another (much less consequential) life, even rise again; but as political actors they will always depend on the services and/or the money of people prepared to push past conventional limits and break rules. Some 400 years later, a compatriot of Machiavelli, Vilfredo Pareto, called them "thrusters." He is mostly remembered for his model of economic change in which everyone gains something ("Pareto optimality")—or, as in promises made by brash promoters of all sorts of plans and products, a win-win outcome. He also wrote about the rise and fall of elites, dividing the world into two constants: a mass of fearful, sluggish "sleepers" clinging to the status quo and an ambitious minority probing for competitive advantage, disturbing the former's slumber and sapping their defences.

In terms of the distinction between societal goods and individual rights, people who prefer contemplative, tranquil and restful good things are at the mercy of people who exercise what they see as their right to pursue Hobbes's "power after power"—or they simply use their powers, aptitudes and talents (or their inherited wealth) without reference to any rights, natural or legal. Their constant goal is a surfeit of power (economic, socio-cultural and political), in order to ensure, at least, continued possession of what they already have. For them, good things are various, mutable, and ever more rapidly changing in response to changes in supply and fashion. Both closed and market economies encourage and reward the invention, manufacture and sale of ever-newer things—and their consumption by as many people as possible, even if that means scavenging landfills of discarded waste. Whatever their philosophy of life or ideology, if any, consumers of this stuff are buried in it. Change is never an unalloyed good thing, but it is inevitable, and the world's thrusters thrive on change and instigate it.

· · · · ·

John Stuart Mill's principle that one person's liberty is limited only by another's is a kind of common-sense utilitarianism—but one that assumes rational individuals ready to compromise on limits. The give-and-take of drawing those lines poses some awkward public-choice questions. Should the market decide whether businesses are punished for refusing to serve blacks and gays? Is there a consensus that a charge of unreasonable discrimination is trumped neither by a sincere belief that racial segregation is of benefit to each segregated race nor by a religious conviction that family values are threatened by open homosexuality? Both positions (only two?) can express a personal distaste for what is seen as unnatural while couching it in the language of principled commitment to the public interest free from any personal bias ("Some of my best friends are gays"). In 1993 the above-profiled Dave Stupich lost his seat in the House of Commons to Reform Party candidate Bob Ringma, who also won unwanted notoriety (causing the party caucus to briefly suspend him) when he opined that small-business owners should be free to fire gay employees if their sexual orientation was disclosed and customers were offended by their presence. He added blacks, saying it would be unfair to not treat all offending minorities the same way. Ringma was a Korean War veteran who served in the Mobile Laundry and Bath Unit, which may explain his electoral success in Nanaimo, home of the world's first bathtub race.

Tastes are never uniform, and they change, which is why the utilitarian goal of the greatest happiness of the greatest number can be understood in different ways by different majorities determined to outlaw different things that they find morally offensive. The issue may then become: which causes more unhappiness to more people, denial or infringement of a right or the social unrest that could result from upholding that right in practice? Government and the law may be called upon, in pursuit of the public interest, to broker a conflict between rights—between a right of public access and a right of, say, religious expression that extends to action or refusal to act. It could (and did) arise in the shape of a baker refusing to design and make a cake for the wedding of a gay couple; the case turned into one of not only his freedom of religious belief that homosexuality is a sin but also his freedom of artistic expression. It could arise in a court of criminal law, in the shape of the right to confront (have access to, see the identifying face of) one's accuser, or prosecution witness in a trial, versus the right (the religious duty perhaps) to always wear full head covering, exposing only the eyes, in public.

It has also arisen in the cancellation of lectures or speeches by people well-known for angry or anger-provoking rhetoric, cancelled because of threatened (or actual) violence in response to announcement of the scheduled speaker and/or the actual speech—and sometimes in response to the response and in support of the speaker. This is a newly familiar example of trying for an accommodation of rights with laws that limit free speech which insults and disrespects minority groups and is a threat to public order. "You can hate any group you wish; just don't broadcast your words." That nostrum has been rendered useless by social media, whose language and visual images claiming to be for a select few (some kind of private "club") are available to anyone online—"Just turn it off if you don't like it [wink, wink, nudge, nudge]." Perpetrators of this stuff want to provoke vengeful ire, and not just among the objects of group hatred and those who commit violence against them; the main target is hate-hunting "progressives." Any carnage resulting from street protest that ends in rioting may or may not have been intended; but laying all the blame for it on those who committed it is like saying someone who likes to stir glowing political embers is not some kind of pyromaniac.

Can the moral principle of respect for persons be extended to groups? Some answer with a resounding yes. It's a safe bet that neither Christ nor Muhammad would care if they heard what infidels said about them; but their followers feel differently. Some Christians bemoan the withering effect of a secular society's toleration of anti- and irreligious talk.

Some American ones have agitated (and some states have enacted laws) in support of strong Christian speech and action in the public square. This may be partly in emulation of the harder line taken by Muslims who seem to believe that anything short of total devotion to their religion poses some kind of existential threat to Islam's position in the world—which prompts the thought that the faith of billions is very fragile indeed if it cannot withstand jokes that have been published about Muhammad. This kind of hypersensitivity is not confined to certain Islamic sects. The knee-jerk reaction to criticism of Israeli policies is to call it anti-Semitic. All of which supports the notion that states aspiring to be religiously, or racially, homogenous harbour totalitarian tendencies that make them inherently dangerous abroad and at home (especially for minorities whose mere presence is a useful pretext for discrimination against an "other" or scapegoat).

In a contest between freedom to speak one's mind and freedom from disrespect, what does disrespect mean? If one or a few members of a group have been singled out for slurs but feel no pain, are self-confident enough to ignore any insult, can the group as a whole demand redress— i.e., have legitimate grounds for saying, in accord with the maxim "one for all, all for one," that the group was made the object of public disrespect and possibly hatred? What about ridicule? What about cartoons? Does context make all the difference between the anti-Semitic drawings (and words) in the *Völkischer Beobachter* and the indirectly anti-Semitic (because critical of Islam by way of its Prophet Muhammad, an Arab Semite) cartoons in *Charlie Hebdo*? The reactions of the offended were very different. Again, context is crucial—very different times and political circumstances. However, murdering the offenders was illegal in both instances. The indiscriminate violence in Paris may be justified by some on the grounds that a whole society is their mortal enemy. It's the kind of belief that tends to be treated as evidence of mental illness, as in the verdict of society (and probably of any prospective jury) on the pilot who murdered 149 other people when he committed suicide by flying an airliner into the French Alps. The Polish-Jewish refugee who assassinated a German diplomat in Paris some 80 years ago, in revenge for the Nazis' anti-Jewish laws, has been excused as insane and then defended as the first Jew to do the kind of thing that many more should have done.

At what point does satirizing tenets of a religious creed and poking fun at aspects of its culture and institutions, when escalated into demeaning the race or ethnicity of its adherents, become incitement to hatred of them that could reasonably be expected to move some of them (and non-adherents, or both) to acts of violence? Jews in Nazi Germany were in no position to protest or resist their treatment, from vile cartoons to state-sanctioned beatings and property theft—and it was too late for any effective defence once deportations began to nobody knew where (except for those directing them). They are hardly in the same predicament, but European Muslims have grounds for thinking that some countries' state apparatus is less concerned about anti-Islamic sentiment and activities than it is about anti-Christian, anti-Jewish and other ethno-religious phobias. There are American individuals and groups openly provoking Islamic backlash, and doing it in the name of freedom of speech. However, they would be the first to seek legal redress, and more, for a cartoon of a Wall Street banker that some might see as an anti-Semitic stereotype; some of them hint at a physically violent attack on Muslims, even if they have said and done nothing objectively provocative. If it is important for a free society to arm itself against murderous offence-takers and the so-called assassin's veto, it is also important that those demanding protection of free speech—for which we all must pay, and not just in monetary terms—exercise some restraint and not go out of their way, and outside the (one hopes, generally agreed) bounds of civil discourse to cause offence, to excite fear and anger. We would do well to keep in mind that, in Alan Ryan's words, "there is a narrow line between asking not to be treated with contempt and asking to be positively valued."

An example of satire producing an oddly mixed (but non-violent) reaction is an Adrian Raeside cartoon in Victoria's daily newspaper. Raeside lampooned the newly elected mayor of the city who, after dropping allegiance to Liz II from the swearing-in ceremony, staged another one on native Indian reserve land in recognition of aboriginal title to a much larger chunk of Victoria. There was unfavourable reaction to the first from supporters of convention and the monarchy. It was overtaken by reaction to the second: congratulatory comment from advanced opinion, quickly followed by an uproar over Raeside's depiction of the event. His clear target was empty gestures. But analysts of his cartoon's cast of characters—which, in addition to officialdom, included hard-hats stomping around the edges (presumably meant to represent developers) and natives in traditional garb—found evidence of neo-colonialism, racism and that all-purpose whipping-boy, disrespect (of which there is plenty to go round, most of it coded, covert and subterranean). Calling attention obliquely to the lack of substantive progress on an issue so vapidly highlighted by the mayoral event brought a deluge of disapproval down on Raeside. He would have received less censure if he had taken on Prime Ministers and their helicopter descents on Indian territory, there dancing the dance of the seven Hudson's Bay blankets, smoking the pipe of peace, then hastily departing with naught to show for their visitation but the show.

Jon Ronson has called attention to what he sees as social media's perverse pleasure in publicly shaming people who cause offence, however inadvertently. The offence may have been felt by very few people—until the shamer drew the public gaze to it. Like surfers of the Net for kinky sex, some tweeters need the fix of taking offence, of finding it where they wanted to find it, and better yet, turning it into group sex. In a radio interview one critic of the Raeside cartoon sounded grateful that it had fallen into the lap of his occupational search for disrespect of aboriginals. Maybe there is something deeper at work: a wish that there not be the sort of offence feared, but needing exorcism of that fear through punishment of those diligently discovered to have committed it—kinky.

— CHAPTER 15 —

Rights and Duties

Immanuel Kant's categorical imperative to "act only in accordance with that maxim through which you can at the same time will that it become a universal law" is one basis for saying that all moral conduct hinges on respect for the dignity of all human beings; and it is what respect for oneself as an autonomous moral being entails. This philosophical version of Christian and other religions' "golden rule" is supposed to work without any religious sanction attached. It has been used in defence of individual freedom of expression against what Mill (following de Tocqueville) called the "tyranny" of majority opinion. Mill moved beyond the strict utilitarianism of its founding father Jeremy Bentham by re-educating himself, especially with respect to, and for, innate moral sentiment (but not Kant's a priori categories that inform all our thinking, including ethical) and intuitive thinking in general. He didn't abandon the greatest happiness principle. He transmuted a societal balance of pleasure over pain into a pursuit of personal fulfillment that entails everyone's freedom from interference in that pursuit. The mutuality of not injuring others in their exercise of such constructive freedom could in itself enlarge everyone's happiness.

Like other Victorian reformers, Matthew Arnold in particular, Mill agitated for educational and other social improvements in the lives of people sunk in poverty, squalor and ignorance. Contemporary cultural conservatives such as F.H. Bradley and J.F. Stephen—and more recent ones such as Gertrude Himmelfarb and Lionel Trilling—argued that Mill showed some failure of moral imagination. For Stephen, a jurist with experience working in India, it was Mill's failure to appreciate the moral fibre sewn into non-European cultures and legal systems that had been an integral part of millions of poor peasant lives for hundreds of years. He compromised, they said, present moral autonomy for the sake of an abstract principle of future societal improvement. He discounted some people's freedom to live a good life as they saw fit—in their familiar unfree circumstances (unfree relative to what, and with what foreseeable increase in freedom capabilities, was unclear)—by questioning their capacity for moral choice (or any choice insofar as it may have moral ramifications).

Before *Ethical Studies* was published in 1876, Francis Herbert Bradley revised it. He conceded it possible for a person of well-grounded moral character to widen his circle of moral obligation to include unfamiliar others, and that widening it to the extent of his becoming a "citizen of the world" need not weaken his moral core. Nevertheless, "My Station and Its Duties" (the cornerstone essay) remained the gold standard— "station" had moved beyond hearth and home, but duties were always more important than rights. As claims of right became more than just declamatory watchwords (as in the French Revolution's "Liberty, Equality, Fraternity"), they were being filled out with demands that could exhaust the most generous and prosperous society's resources. Liberty and equality are very expansive principles.

When Thomas Stearns Eliot left St. Louis, hotbed of American Hegelianism, to study abroad, he chose Bradley as his dissertation subject.

However, philosophical idealism and its Oxford home were losing the battle for hearts and minds to a kind of neo-Platonist banquet being prepared at Cambridge by G.E. Moore, Bertrand Russell and Ludwig Wittgenstein—one where Bradley could have played the Spirit of Christmas Past (or Banquo's ghost). Bradley argued that our sense of right and wrong is formed from childhood learning by concrete example. It teaches not human rights but our duties of care and courtesy to one another. These duties can also be carried out through collective response to the human condition of the disabled, the deranged and the destitute. Furthermore, Mr. Moore, the contemplation of pure truth, beauty and love is a different thing entirely than doing the right thing.

On the contemporary world stage, we see pictures of soldiers in full combat gear (accessorized with high-tech instruments making them look like Martian invaders), who have been sent by "freedom-loving" countries to lecture Muslim peoples on the benefits of progress and human rights. This has been, to put it mildly, a severe test of their religiously ordained duty of hospitality to strangers. Putting it bluntly, the latter's duty is to be good guests while they mind their own real, bloody business, which is to hunt terrorists—mixing with civilians who have reason to distrust both indiscriminate terrorists and the ones trying to discriminate in hunting them. Most foreign soldiers have voluntarily submitted to strict performance of military duty—to which the countries that send them add social work, economic development and political education, a sure-fire recipe for PTSD. Leaders of those countries may descend by helicopter to reassure the troops with talk of their brave defence of their countries' values. The public relations side of this "mission" is led by "brass" who have to somehow contrive to make it complement the military side, both of which the "poor bloody infantry" has to carry out. Quite apart from the mounting veterans' affairs ("wounded warriors") deficit and coalition leaders' blundering intervention in areas they know very little about (and whose native leadership can't or won't get them to understand), they have a duty to explain why their countries are obliged to carry the "war on terrorism" to countries already in civil-war conditions, besieged by contending religious and ideological fanatics, foreign and domestic. Fighting them "over there," so we won't have to defend our shores and homes, seems clever until we count the cost: our dead and maimed heroes are far outnumbered by "over there" civilian casualties directly attributable to our intervention. Almost the only time one hears mention of this "collateral damage" is when it's safe to blame it on some evil genius, such as the Iranian special-ops general "we" cleverly assassinated.

President Trump has decided to solve the "Middle East problem" by doing what worked for him as a businessman: buy 'em off. The military option is too expensive (apart from its flag-hugging patriotism dividend). Diplomacy takes too long and is too hard on the brain. So why not offer them American-style prosperity? Just look at Israel, beneficiary of U.S. mega-bucks, (some of) which Palestinians too could get. We got a foretaste of this tactic (strategy is too grand a word for it) when early in Trump's courtship of Kim he dangled in the dictator's face the prospect of tourism on North Korean beaches. Arab nations (some of them crippled from birth by Anglo-French C-sections) admittedly need help; but it has to arrive under UN auspices to have any chance of doing any good. And that could mean attaching UN human rights and International Court of Justice strings to the assistance. Some of them are not nation-states in any normal sense but hereditary monarchies based on tribal fiefdom; and many contain minorities they are trying to subjugate if not expel. One conflict the West has serious skin in is the Israeli-Palestinian one, if only because of Israel's grip on U.S. public opinion. Mitigation, of international tension at least, could begin by U.S. governments penalizing each new Israeli expropriation of lands long occupied and cultivated by Palestinians.

. . . . .

Moral choice moments can occur in less urgent and less public situations, while revealing a political dimension in all ethical choices. Deciding whether or not to tell a lie in order to spare another person's feelings may cause momentary, and telltale, hesitation. This is not a problem for President Trump, although he does exhibit a fondness for firing people at a distance or telling an aide to deliver the bad news, which raises doubts about the strength of his convictions. Also, he doesn't tell lies. To be a liar, one has to know the difference between truth and falsehood. He simply assumes that whatever comes out of his mouth or tweeter is *ipso facto* the truth. Returning to the quandary, you may have time for the agonizing luxury of weighing the options: tell him the unvarnished truth, consult and co-opt other people to help deliver it—always a favourite—or sweeten it. Which, done with or without others' help, will probably make him resentful of people thinking he needs to be fed the proverbial spoonful of sugar and left in the dark about the offence given, mistake made, misfortune suffered, or whatever the unpalatable truth is. An instinct to be brutally direct with the truth has the saving grace of lancing the boil of suspicion before it grows a nasty head. But the urge to put off the awkward moment, in the hope that it becomes somebody else's problem, or is postponed indefinitely by intervening events, is more powerful. You may think about what you should do as a rule, according to some categorical imperative, and about what would make you at least appear consistent and feel more comfortable in your moral skin. A self-serving motive creeps back in: you are thinking about others' reactions to your conduct—including the one who is the object of the quandary; you are its self-conscious subject—and not what God, St. Augustine or Immanuel Kant might say.

The internal debate that arises in moral dilemmas is a form of politics, in the sense of trying to end up with a decision that reconciles as many of the competing options or points of view as possible—in and for one head or among and for many. We are moving into areas and situations where sensitivity to personal feelings yields ground to adjudication. How, say, can colleagues be brought to resolve an issue among them in which one claims, with evidence, that another is spending far too much time helping new staff and not enough on production? Her help, she claims, is making a contribution to a better future pace of production. But the most pressing need is maintaining output, which requires maximum effort by experienced staff members. With the added complication of no love lost between the competing claimants, it can be assumed that settling the matter by themselves is a non-starter, even when told to do so, and how to do so, by the boss of what has always been a collegial workplace. What about a staff meeting? A predictable mixed result is (a) loss of collegiality; (b) a sense of grievance on the part of both claimants—in part because other permanent staff members try too hard to be impartial, feeling somehow compelled to sit in judgment—and further animosity between the two as well as against hoped-for allies; and (c) an unstated decision, inferred from some of their actions, to expend less energy on monitoring others' work and more on their own. A compromise has been achieved, not without (some lasting) pain, some (or one) of which will go away over time.

— CHAPTER 16 —

Lies, Damn Lies and History

The liberal-democratic public opinion victory for human rights and
the idea that individual self-fulfillment is the primary vessel for social
excellence of all kinds continues to confront insurgent and resurgent
collective identity politics, some based on religion, some ethno-racist
and some extremely militant. Some of it is an attack on rapid globalization facilitated by communications and other information technology—
which is used by two kinds of enemy of an increasingly interconnected
and intersected world to try to undermine that world. The objective of
the first's efforts bears an uncanny resemblance to 1871 *communards* at-
tacking public clocks in Paris in order to stop the uneven, unequal progress of the world by stopping the despotic rule of timing machines.
That's the Luddite wing of resistance to the World Wide Web, and its
members are adept users of what they attack—the bombs they throw
are electronic and hard to trace. The other wing wants to conserve a
wired but wireless world apparatus in support of its narrow purpose:
undermining cultural miscegenation (as they regard increasing population diversity in advanced Western nations caused by "liberal" immigration policies). This reaction is not confined to Western nations.

Japan, China and India are highly (or, in the case of India, relatively) advanced industrial nations that "defend" themselves against racial and religious heterogeneity. In the case of China and India, extreme and even violent measures are used. In India's case, it's a legacy of the British Raj, its partition and (partial) expulsion of Muslims; and their expulsion from Burma, a neighbouring multi-ethnic imperial remnant. Bangladesh, the former East Pakistan and next-door neighbour, is reluctant for a variety of reasons to admit these fellow Muslims violently ejected by officially and rigidly Buddhist Burma, now Myanmar; but the humanitarian willingness of thousands of impoverished Bangladeshis to take them in is an example that shames the rest of us. What all these defensive nationalisms have in common (to varying degrees) is lost content, an imagined past golden age, and a burning desire to "make [blank] great again." In some other, smaller countries, there is a fear of being demographically overrun by indirect force of arms (e.g., the Baltic states when they were Soviet satellites), by some large minority's "revenge of the cradle" or by the explosive refugee crisis.

Historiography is the not so hidden problem here—or rather, history as memory, which on its own can make for badly written history. One of the bastard offspring of the Web is the multi-viral contagion of social media platforms. Under cover of the right to free speech, a phantasmagoria of historical mis- and disinformation, including conspiracy theories about historical events, has infected cyberspace, and is universally accessible. A lot of it is written by people with a very reactionary axe to grind. Reliable histories, written by respected, diligent historians, are also available online; but they involve some mental effort, and "suggested further reading." The quick and easy stuff, saying what some people want to read, and no more, is more accessible. One of the goals of the "new historiography" is to simplify memory by eliminating nuance and creating a single orthodox story line. Tara Westover's *Educated*, her memoir of family life with a fundamentalist Mormon father and her flight from Idaho to a Cambridge PhD in history, is particularly good on extracting an accurate account of the past from conflicting family memories. She has many insightful things to say about human memory mistakes and the magnetic power of (in her case, family) myth. Her mind is torn between what she is sure of, first confirmed and later recanted by some of her siblings, and hard-wired loyalty to the very different collective memory of the rest of the family, assiduously re-inforced and polished, as directed by its patriarch.

Critical history tells us that collective memory is, strictly speaking, psychologically impossible. There can be shared memories, but no such thing as one big, common mind—a mind-set, maybe, which is, fashionably speaking, a social construct; more contentiously, a myth. Every long-lasting social group has what is sometimes called an official history, one that tries to squeeze the experiences of minorities into the container of the prevailing narrative. It stresses a group's struggle to survive natural disaster, foreign invasion, internal subversion or (particularly now) globalization in every form: primarily technological, then commercial-financial and cultural. New things happen—including the discovery of "old" facts—at a faster and faster pace; and societies try to keep up by reconstructing their traditions. This is where much-maligned "alternative facts" have a role to play. (Merriam-Webster offers guarded support for Kellyanne Conway's use of "alternative" to mean "other" facts. But to say that a photo of 10,000 people is really a picture of 100,000, which President Trump continues to say of his inauguration audience, is not to state another or additional fact but to make an addition mistake.) Slave memories are different than those of former slave-owners, as with aboriginal experience versus colonist and settler experience, and dissenters and resisters versus compromisers and collaborators. Their different stories both interact and conflict; they have misapprehensions about each other; and they all have their own martyrs and monuments, but differing versions of heroism, military, political and moral. National identities are sustained by regular reminders of a nation's glorious past (or grievance, as Kosovo is for Serbs). But the more they are commemorated, the more they are open to questioning, investigation and revision. New-old facts may provoke violent reactions from self-appointed custodians of treasured memories—nobody can be allowed to forget. Simon Jenkins has said that to stop drinking "at the rancid well of grievance…some compromise between present and past" must be found. That could mean a lot of forgetting—more morally questionable than forgiving, but politically necessary, says David Rieff in his *In Praise of Forgetting*, a book about, among much else, converting a particular history into a weapon for winning a political argument. This is selective history, which includes trying to rebut an example of one wrongdoing with a series of events that for some is a mnemonic for all wrongdoing: "Clinton lied!" "What about Watergate? Nixon screwed the whole country."

That a government should try to induce forgetting sounds Orwellian. Why not leave Confederate statues up, unprotected from protest graffiti and other disfigurement? Regular attacks followed by repair could be the occasion for free and democratic debate—learning moments leading to further study, and the whole Jim Crow false memory being put to bed with the light on and the heat off. The same applies to the monuments and revisionist histories of such Canadian figures as Cornwallis, savage discriminator against Nova Scotia aboriginals; even statues of John A. Macdonald, "Father" of Canadian Confederation, have been threatened with removal. Why not make a statue trio of Macdonald, George Étienne Cartier, the largely forgotten other "Father," and Louis Riel, the one who rebelled against the official version? But the urge to impose a cultural order, moral as well as political—which entails the writing and teaching of (only) official, orthodox history—is an ancient one, has never lost its grip on the political imagination, and many governments have been seduced by it. Like D.H. Lawrence's

"Humming-Bird…far back, in some otherworld, primeval-dumb, it raced down the avenues…/Probably he was big…a jabbing, terrifying monster/We look at him through the wrong end of the long telescope of time/Luckily for us." However, our luck is running out; we need to look in the rear-view mirror as well as through a telescope. Myth-making—which we like to think we've left far behind—is the ante-room to mythomania, a fancy name for repeated lying. We don't need historiography to know that the bigger the lie, the more likely it is to be believed: "He wouldn't have said something so incredible if it weren't true."

— CHAPTER 17 —

Political Ethics and Role-Playing

Introspection, that hardy perennial of philosophical argument about the true nature of human nature, is a treasure trove of evidence for ambiguity and fluidity in self-knowledge and identity. Jurisprudence and psychiatry depend upon, respectively, establishing and re-establishing stability of personhood. Yet the testimony of both witnesses and patients indicates that many of them are to varying degrees uncertain whether what they say they remember as their firsthand experience is indeed so. A person can appropriate parts of others' experiences and make them his own—by and large, women are less prone to this kind of romancing. It is in part a matter of experiences (one's own and others') becoming ever more credible as they are told and retold. This may include "stories" (family history as remembered or literary stories as read) that encapsulate, typecast and mentally engrave examples of all kinds of human behaviour, often with the aid of vivid pictorial images. It can involve reconstruction and renovation that make an event both more memorable and more objective (in the sense of conforming to what others say they recall).

In most public business, living in and out of an alternative universe (or more than one) is not an accepted time-out—although that and other kinds of nuance, and allowances made for good intentions and instances of "good behaviour," can play a part in criminal justice sentencing, a cause for loud protest. An alternative verdict, and sentence, for being mentally somewhere else when the offence took place is, to use U.K. idiom, being "sectioned" for some kind (to be determined) of insanity. Most people manage to keep themselves together enough to function at work and in society, and play the roles expected of them there. Nevertheless, at different times and to varying degrees, people imagine what might have been and what might be, and create alternative characters, lives and careers for themselves.

Ronald Reagan, some say, was too long a Hollywood actor who played too many roles. Here he is apologizing for the Iran-Contra affair: "A few months ago I told the American people I did not trade arms for hostages. My heart and my best intentions still tell me that's true, but the facts and the evidence tell me it is not." Unlike President Trump, he was prepared to admit that there were facts that could defeat his best (or any) intentions. William Empson, pre-eminent investigator of literary ambiguity, said that people "will have still lingering in their minds the way they would have preserved their self-respect if they had acted differently…they are only to be understood by bearing both possibilities [which they were in some way prepared to do] in mind." Trump will have none of that wish-washy nonsense. No ambiguity for him: the facts are simply what he says they are. Intentions are irrelevant. Impulsive, unreflective action (of which he is a master) is sufficient and necessary; and it seems to have mastered him and his presidency. In *The Illuminations* Andrew O'Hagan says we learn "over the miles…how to read a person by finding what character was available." There are grounds for wondering whether Trump has any character at all left in his bag of tricks. His overbearing persona seems to have conquered whatever personhood he may have had at one time.

His long success bullying and threatening people who impede his business career (in both senses of the word "career") has made it hard for him to take his political opponents seriously. He can't understand constitutionally based inquiries into his presidential conduct. He used to be able to block, elude or outlast his "enemies." Now they're playing games. He's like the brute confronting the cinematic Butch Cassidy and asking "Rules?!" The result for Trump has been similar, but by a rulebook, which someone should read to him. Auditioning for the lead role in some movie about some president, he wrote a post-production script for the aborted Ukraine deal, which he read to a press scrum, while pacing (treading the boards?) and repeatedly shouting the words "no quid pro quo." He said he looked forward to a Senate trial—one in which he could play the part of a fighter for people dismissed by Beltway elites as "deplorables." President Trump is a figment of Donald Trump's imagination. So what's to impeach? Only a very bad actor.

To have a moral character of any kind one must, says Bradley, accumulate habits of conduct that are part of a coherent identity. It would be inhuman to expect another person to be literally predictable, like water freezing at zero degrees Celsius. On the other hand, without some measure of consistency in conduct, a person will be shunned as unreliable and irresponsible. Donald Trump's unpredictability fetish looks increasingly like cover for absence of background study and other preparatory thinking, if not, as some opponents allege, absence of any moral sense. It may be considered smart, in social life and business as well as in the politicking arts, to avoid telegraphing one's intentions; but short of hostile engagement, of actually being at war, reliability is necessary for both domestic tranquillity and international peace. Trump's words and his administration's actions look like two distinct and very loosely connected spheres of incoherence.

He tells what the Brits call porkies, archly greasing them with escape clauses: "People are saying"; "There was more good Wikileaks stuff. I love Wikileaks, but I don't want to keep you waiting." He finally, in his own mind, ended the "birther" rumour that Obama was born in Kenya (and therefore illegally elected President)—Trump didn't start it, but kept fanning the flames long after it had been thoroughly discredited. He concluded his brief statement ("I, Donald J. Trump, now end this rumour") by leaning into the cameras with his signature smug grin and adding: "If you know what I mean." ("We're not sure we do know what you mean, Donald. We have reason to believe it is something you would rather not tell us and we would rather not hear.") His insinuations call to mind the Monty Python skit in which a man is sitting alone in a pub enjoying a quiet pint, and another man sidles over to him and abruptly says: "I bet your wife's a real goer. Know what I mean, know what I mean." The first man is understandably taken aback and at a loss for words. Eric Idle(r the Sidler) leans in: "Say no more, say no more." Art foreshadowed Trump making a joke of his inflammatory language, followed by his flunkies telling us to "not take him literally, take him seriously," and the press to "shut up and listen."

Trump is a master of the art of non-standard deviation, diverting attention from one empty claim of success to the next, and from responsibility for his administration's mistakes and for his presidential lies. He made a literally (and seriously) incredible attempt to have people believe that his unfounded accusation that President Obama authorized a wiretap of Trump Tower was based on media reports and not started by one of his own tweets: " Don't ask me whether it's true, ask Fox News." This may be a symptom of factitious disorder (often called Munchausen's) syndrome by proxy (see chapter 21). The press he berates for lying about him has turned into his proxy self, a Charlie McCarthy to his Edgar Bergen. Journalists are manipulated, in part by their own commitment to accuracy, into reporting his endless stream of distortions verbatim;

and then, when as good reporters they question his veracity, he points to all their reports as evidence in support of what he said: "Everybody is talking about it." The "lame-stream" press, hastened and hobbled by an antiquated commitment to discovering all the Trump truth they can, are left bemused in the wake of his muse of nonsense and the devilishly inspired tricks of Trumpe d'oreille.

A guest on BBC's "Hard Talk" said, as a kind of afterthought, that Trump could be considered a "self-baiting satirist." Like archetypal American con man P.T. Barnum, Trump has fooled the people of his so-called base into thinking they can't be fooled. They're in on the joke; they laugh knowingly when they applaud his crudities. He's just throwing them out to see what happens. When rally crowds are entertained by his political improvisations, there is mutual confirmation that they know something the disbelievers do not. If one of them—such as calling himself a stable genius—fails to resonate with his followers, but becomes a source of general mirth, he drops it from his routine.

In an interview with NBC's Lester Holt, Trump said: "I said to myself, I said, you know, this Russia thing is a made-up story." Note that three people are already involved. But he talks to his mirror image; unlike most people, Trump doesn't have an alter ego that stores, among other things, a bad conscience. Nor does he have a superego, essential for socialization. Talking to his ego trumps all other dialogue (pun intended). Holt or anybody else who sits down at this card table is assumed by the dealer to have agreed to Trump rules. Note the look of despairing resignation on the face of almost any truth-seeking interviewer of Trump after they realize they'll never wring it out of him. "You know" is more than just a speech tic; it's axiomatic, because three people (one of whom can be a Trump rally crowd) are in syllogistic agreement—Trump's version of political triangulation.

— CHAPTER 18 —

"as freedom is a breakfastfood"

The debate between neo-conservative moral freedom and liberal social betterment continues into the information age and knowledge economy. We're now told we are at a stage of social development that requires continual learning, mental upgrades designed to infuse us with new ways of thinking and communicating, so that people of all kinds and classes are able to live a decent life. But all this re-education needs quantity control and quality assurance. Or do people make their own trial-and-error way through the sales-pitch maze of instruction and equipment—with the help of next-gen family members who are *au courant*, in the swim with (Gordon) Moore's law of IT novelty followed by almost immediate obsolescence? Can learners be "nudged" toward self-enlightenment by "libertarian paternalism" (Cass Sunstein) directing them to knowledge that helps them make (their own) better-informed choices that will improve their lives? This smacks of social engineering according to some appointed or self-appointed group's values. Choices are to be framed by some "choice architecture"—words that suggest a penthouse or *de haut en bas* attitude, and (some say) infantilization of the choosers.

The first question is about technical competence and ability to navigate the digital universe. The second raises supplementary questions about a so-called revolution in human relationships of every kind (social, workplace and recreational) brought about by technology—not the devices and apps, but the basic science of artificial intelligence, and what that means for what we think we know about human nature.

The happy talk about all the things that robots will do for us as if they were us has an undertone of nervous laughter. Some pioneers of the digital wave that some others are triumphantly surfing have long been sounding concerns if not outright alarms. One unpleasant actuality that has attracted a lot of attention, including public debate about what can be done to regulate it in the public interest, is broadcast of malign mis- and disinformation that calls itself free speech. Whether it be foreign meddling in another nation's electoral process or entirely home-grown political dirty tricks, or at another level entirely, luring vulnerable people, especially children, into activities that expose them to public humiliation and, worse, loss of liberty and life in some criminal underworld, the only remedy is education—one that cannot be found entirely online. Sorry, kids, you need to read a book or three, some of which you will probably be able to find online. But do you know what to look for? Younger kids should be encouraged to hear, or read, cautionary "fairy" tales like *Hansel and Gretel*. Older kids should know that an important defence against Net malpractice is ad skepticism. We all know by now that Web and Net are names that can mean snare or trap more than support and security. Reading scholarly histories—they're not all dull—can impart useful as well as interesting knowledge about our technology, culture, government, economy and politics.

Another digital downside is the ease with which people's vital stats can be poached from the fair-game reserve. Net service providers mine the petabytes of data that Net users automatically cough up, and sell it to marketers and other advertisers. It is carelessly provided (in some cases free of charge) to self-described researchers of public opinion, who share their data analysis with political opinion makers, for whom knowledge is power—and clients' money, some of which they kick back to their academic suppliers. By aggregating their users' postings, Facebook and other social media giants have built what Nicholas Carr calls "digital sharecropping." Users "operate happily in an attention economy" that is "just a means of creating cheap inputs for the [plantation owners'] cash economy." The used users are 'appily appy, proud players in a so-called sharing economy that rewards them with gratification for their "letting" others "share" their houses through Airbnb and for using Uber's freelance taxi drivers and other allegedly self-employed contractors.

There are two more no-free-lunch realities. One is government surveillance by way of its access to Net users' personal information through its own and corporate data-collating algorithms. What was thought to be private information is used by both the private and the public sector to deny people what they were led to believe they were going to get. And, of course, there is illegal hacking into all networks, government and non-government, for criminal profit-making purposes as well as spurious public service ones—not to mention vandalism and other gratuitous mischief-making.

Not so gratuitous is the instantaneously worldwide transmission of half-truths and falsehoods by malign governmental as well as non-governmental Internet players in a no-holds-barred free-for-all that too many treat as one more convenience store that is also, somehow, a low- or no-cost community service. But most of this information highway has no lanes, verges or fencing, no directional signage and no traffic lights. Inevitably, it has been taken over by characters out of *Mad Max*.

. . . . .

The old (and trite) debate between "negative freedom from" and "positive freedom to" and about whether freedom is more than absence of restraint on movement—in person, in occupation, in trade (of property or ideas)—has been set aside by global awareness of a widespread, striking lack of fundamental freedom from hunger, disease, maiming and death: every disaster of war for millions of people in today's world. This should not be compared to WWII—this is the result of (un)civil war caused by natural resource (land and water) degradation and depletion, and of old and new religious and ideological fundamentalism. Paraphrasing Philip ("Dante on an empty stomach") Wicksteed, it's hard to appreciate life-fulfilling things when you and your family are starving in a bombed-out house or, up a notch, an unwanted charity case in a refugee camp. Opposed to them are people who see such distress as a threat to their freedom to enjoy their higher freedoms. How else explain fear of the downtrodden, even when the unfree ones are nowhere near? But everybody and everything is nearer now; and global communication makes the heart-rending quality of images of chronic distress inseparable from their fear-mongering utility.

Was Thomas Hobbes a fearmonger? He is known for asserting that fear is the most powerful human motive—fear of death, not of death itself but of being knocked out of the human race, which is a race for power and fame. It's also a fear of not being there for what will happen next, for what those still around, above ground, will be doing and saying ("about me"). He did paint an unflattering picture of the human psyche: fear of others' power balanced by self-delusion about one's own; and "...the characters of man's heart, blotted and confounded as they are with dissembling, lying, counterfeiting, and erroneous doctrines, are legible only to him who searcheth hearts"—but "he that reads is himself a good or evil man," because it's human nature to adopt "characters" or roles that disguise one's true character (*Leviathan*, Intro. and ch. 8). Oh well, cheer up, and as David Hume advised 100 years later, take a brisk walk, have some small talk, a loaf of bread, a jug of wine, and thou beside me singing…. Oh, sorry, that was some Persian called Omar Khayyam.

High on Hobbes's list of dissembling words was "liberty," when used to arouse the passions of people otherwise at their ease. The libertarian braying of people who are competing to wield power for, they trumpet, protection of a higher way of life is reminiscent of an acid comment made by Samuel Johnson at an early stage of the American colonial rebellion: "Why do we hear the loudest yelps for liberty from drivers of negroes?" We now hear the same hypocritical bombast from people arming themselves to the teeth: "The only defence against a bad guy with a gun is a good guy with a gun"—as if "good" guys were readily identifiable, and reliable, in the usual chaos of mass shootings. They fear latent state power's imagined threat to enact an imagined majority's wish to confiscate all guns. The proponents of some measure(s) of gun control fear the apparent inability of that power to fulfill its side of a contract to secure the lives—and non-gun freedoms—of a citizen majority that does not want gun power to rule. The increasing militarism of para-military police forces in the U.S. (and in Canada to a lesser extent) is a product of accelerating symbiosis between soldiering, policing and Hollywood movies that glorify "action" men (and women). Policing is depicted as all about destroying evil people. Police who serve their communities in more peaceful ways are mostly cast in romantic comedies. (1) The job of police officer seems to attract people inclined and/or used to violence. (2) If they want to be warriors, they should enlist and serve under a uniform code of conduct, be subject to military discipline; unions are only for pay and benefits. (3) Civilian guns should be subject to confiscation—the mental fitness test for gun ownership is a bad joke; every human being has fits of berserker rage.

There is a depressing amount of contemporary evidence that people of exceptional power and influence are able to (a) trust other people to trust them even as they (b) commit outrageous acts of deceit and betrayal. In Hobbesian terms, we can never be free of the fear that others entertain the same malevolent and predatory thoughts as us. Pride in one's superior ability to overcome obstacles that defeat other men is a product of life in any human society, but especially in one where enough people enjoy enough competitive advantage for illusions of lasting superiority to flourish and grow into self-delusion. Such "needy men, and hardy, not contented with their present condition" are not *in* need or material want; they have insatiable appetites that can only be contained, and only by sovereign political power.

—CHAPTER 19—

Au Café du Grand-commun

Jean-Jacques Rousseau irritated a wide spectrum of Enlightenment opinion—and he still does; but "progressive" and New Age opinion have absorbed him. His fellow foes of the not so *ancien régime* of church and state, *les philosophes*, expelled him from their fellowship when they realized that he was a very different sort of thinker than they had thought. In the grimly minatory *Reflections on the Revolution in France*, he is a member of Edmund Burke's rogues' gallery of revolutionary opinion-makers, but a bit of a misfit in that pantheon. Sharp-tongued Dr. Samuel Johnson angrily denounced him as an obnoxious hypocrite. When the French Catholic Church banned and burned his "Creed of a Savoyard Priest," accusing him of propagating pantheism, and forced him into exile, *le bon* David Hume came to his aid and offered him asylum. He quickly became a very unwelcome guest. Famous for his sweet nature and even temper, Hume found himself participating in the sort of defamatory gossip that was a staple of Rousseau's literary relationships.

Rousseau was no academic, but the first of his two discourses, "on the Sciences and Arts," won the Prize of the Academy of Dijon. It said two things sure to please any establishment: that the new "enlightened" thinking was inimical to virtue; and that morals were deteriorating, compared to (some of) the good old days. His second, on the "Origins and Foundations of Inequality Among Men," was less well received. He said moral decline ran deeper than a claque of rationalist scribblers. It's the human condition in settled societies, particularly in those that encourage and facilitate dis-play. This is not about the (presumed) innocence of children's play; it is more than play when it becomes a platform for comparison and critical assessment, and then for envy and resentment. Much of the blame, says Rousseau, can be laid at the gate of the first man to fence off a piece of land and claim it as his own, his exclusive property. Acts of enclosure gave rise to what is now known as a long revolution. Subsistence agriculture was overtaken by large-scale and surplus production; barter for need lost ground to excessive, conspicuous consumption; and more social room (time) was made for leisurely learning and salons (space) for fashionable display of wit at others' expense, a frequent target of Rousseau's ire. Rousseau's perspicacity is not diminished by the fact that in his day the vast majority of Europeans lived on and from the land, which was not theirs, and even if it was, they possessed few material chattels. They were sunk in "rural idiocy" (Karl Marx)—which calls for two comments: (a) idiocy originally did not mean stupidity but isolation from wider human contact (the ancient Athenian "idiotes" lived among many others but refused to pay any attention to them, a form of self-imposed stupidity); (b) European peasants, and others, fled to America more for free land than for religious freedom.

The evolution from living well enough to living large gave rise to a tectonic shift from natural empathy or fellow feeling to reflective moral judgment. As soon as human beings began to ask, "What should I, or we, do in this situation?"—rather than instinctively come to the aid and comfort of others, or not, depending on the dictates of simple self-preservation—

the serpent of calculation entered this internal debate: "What moral code is in vogue with people I need, or wish, to impress? Shall I ingratiate myself in return for future favour(s) or lack of disfavour? Will doing the conventionally honourable thing turn me into an object of ridicule, or not doing it, an object of obloquy?"; and as a last resort, "Will I be able to live with myself if I ignore my conscience?"

As an *étranger*, an outsider, living (from time to time) in *le haut monde*, Rousseau could claim to be a keener observer of it than were those sunk in their slavery to fashion. He detected the real culprit and the real victim—one and the same, of course. Human beings are fearful of change, even of improvements in their living conditions. At the same time they are infatuated with and covetous of them when enjoyed by others. Socio-economic drivers (the main one now an advertising industry that promotes novelty) combine with political power (in hock to market forces, and as unwilling as it is unable to resist them) to make it difficult for individuals to hold onto a stable, independent identity. Fashionable has replaced reliable in goods and services, and in human character. Natural self-love free of affectation, *amour de soi*, has mutated into love of what it is socially appropriate to eat, wear, say, think and do, *amour propre*. It is a new kind of self-love, a creature of public opinion and the pressures exerted by *le grand commun*.

· · · · ·

That sounds like the "great society" (LBJ) or the "big society" (U.K. PM David Cameron), both slogans for promoting something that, in the second example, was never more than a catchword. For Rousseau, it was a cafeteria of idle chit-chat, or in present-day terms, a supermarket display of packaged goods that are all about the bottle, can or cardboard come-on and of no substantial worth. The more talk there is of a "just society," the more people suspect yet more flimflam. One of the few who seriously tried to cost her reforms, Senator Warren, could not persuade enough voters to support her in the Democratic presidential primary. The impatience of supporters of her and Senator Sanders is understandable. It is almost 30 years since the Clinton administration tried to put a public option, if not single-(tax)payer basic health care, on the legislative (for eventual delivery to the kitchen) table, during which time private health-care insurance became less affordable or even available.

Have most people in the U.S. resigned themselves to careful step-by-step progress towards the goal of a society with more equal opportunities—the RBG (Ruth Bader Ginsburg) approach that President Obama seemed to be (somewhat tentatively) embarked upon? Shocked by the 2010 mid-term election results, he replaced further expenditure on health care, housing and other social infrastructure with deficit reduction—which (predictably) didn't stop Republicans continuing to unite around agreeing to "just say no" to everything proposed by his administration and to focus all their efforts on whatever could deny him a second term. As for the Patient Protection and Affordable Care Act, they kept hitting the repeal button in knee-jerk reaction to any and all proposed amendments. Rather than proffer advice (in the spirit of senatorial "advise and consent") to a duly elected head of the executive branch, the GOP played a relentlessly partisan game, even in foreign policy where, as is said ad nauseam, partisanship is supposed to stop at the water's edge. In Hobbes's words, there was "one or more amongst them that desire to have him lose"—as if it were not enough that the administration "wheelbarrow" is "heavy of itself and retarded by the inconcurrent judgments and endeavours of them that drive it..." (*Leviathan*, ch. 25). The GOP dog whistle turned into a bull horn "Get the black man out of the white house"—a modern American Battle of the White Mountain, followed not by the Defenestration of Prague but by Denigration on the Potomac.

One thing neither Hobbes nor anyone else could have foreseen was the elevation of a political novice into legitimate ruler of a global hegemon, multitudes of whose citizens hungered to believe his humbuggery. There's more to the Democrat critique and Republican neo-federalist defence of Donald Trump's victory in 2016 than a dispute over the difference between national popular-vote numbers and state-by-state Electoral College ones. Presidential political legitimacy concerns, including Trump's own, are about more than the effect of Russian electoral interference. They also involve a belief that to have political legitimacy one must pass two tests: political experience and performance; and, through them, the degree to which one has gained and retained any moral authority.

One of Trump's key advisers, Steven Miller, has called the President a "political genius," on the basis of his unexpected 2016 victory. He won because his campaign exploited an opening made by Lady Misfortune. The gap Hillary Clinton's opponent slipped through was her (and other Democrats) taking for granted one of their traditional bases: the (mostly white) industrial working class, whose middle-class aspirations have been thwarted for over a generation by forces of change that no government has been able or willing to mitigate. It didn't matter that he was a boastful billionaire playboy who claimed, with truly awesome chutzpah, that his personal indebtedness made him uniquely qualified to manage the American economy, nor that she was more qualified by governmental experience to be President. Incoherent anger at disparate, ill-defined elites made just enough people eager to vote for a demon of disorder rather than a political fixer. Trump tapped into a deep pop-cultural reservoir of repressed inbred prejudice; and he continues to sow seeds of discord that he claims, paradoxically, only he can heal. And the Joker continues to re-live and re-relish his victory over Batwoman.

. . . . .

Getting back to *amour propre* and *le grand commun*, in *Émile*, a "treatise on education," Rousseau propounds a cure for over-socialized man, who "confuses time, place, and natural conditions"—a variation on Hobbes's distinction between man's basic nature (which he sees as an insatiable appetite for power and glory) and the effect of differing social conditions on precisely how that nature manifests itself. Rousseau's remedy for moral confusion begins with removal of the child from society, from familiar (and familial) surroundings, and his seclusion in a place dedicated to educing his potential for natural feelings. (For girls, there was a novel, *Julie, ou la Nouvelle Héloïse*, which contains advice on political economy as well as what used to be called home economics.) Rousseau's pedagogy is quite strict and authoritarian for someone widely considered a libertine: "From the outset build a wall around your child's soul." Because of its doctrinaire curriculum and boarding-school trappings, his methods seem more like training than education, and artificial insofar as the man must eventually be returned to society. The ethic of his education will, Rousseau says, inoculate the child against fads and flattery, and prepare him for citizenship. (Like so many other such programs, including the constitutions he wrote for Poland and Corsica, we should read them as what are now called thought experiments.) If children are not raised in the prescribed way, as adults they will be in thrall to the enticements of *le grand commun*. Anxiety about how others see them will make them look at themselves only through others' eyes; and they will fear the social death of not fitting in. They will lose any sense of having an independent self, the ability to know who they are, the foundation of moral will power. (With or without his "method," Rousseau's conclusions helped inspire Kant and his most influential work, *Critique of Practical* [i.e., ethical] *Reason*).

It remains as true today as it was in the efflorescence of the Italian Renaissance that wealth and beauty (or glamour), commercial and artistic success and patronage of the arts can enhance, even create, political fame. There's an underlying continuity in the repeated emergence of eras in which the clamorous presentation of a leisure class and its stuff, media exposure (a latecomer) and political ambition make for a mutual admiration society. In our new Gilded Age, Donald Trump, sometime socialite and World Wrestling Entertainer (political rally division), is a non-starter in the arts patronage and philanthropy category and a bit *nouveau riche*. Celebrity's political dimension is an integral part of the endless news cycle and media demand for opinion filler. The matching desire to be a newsmaker is so great that some Mafia dons have let their religion of *omerta* lapse, opining on society's ills while confessing to their own part in them—this before being actually charged with any-thing (in a fit of pre-indictment plea-bargaining?). Interviews with elected representatives and other opinion leaders turn into frenetic sound-bite warfare; the opinions of movie stars and rock musicians begin to sound more thoughtful and balanced than those of their pre-sumed betters. Whether they speak cracker-barrel philosophy, sonorous legalese, bureaucratic bafflegab or schoolyard insult, they all share an irresistible urge to attract attention and be in the limelight, however lurid. Awe- or adoration-inspiring figures (or, if inspiration falters, in-timidating ones) are put on a pedestal (at a table or behind a lectern in front of network TV). Others' envious desire to see them fall into spec-tacular disgrace is a by-product of their sudden fame and prestige.

In today's *grand commun* people bounce off one another in a mad social whirl, in search of both distraction and attention. They want to know, but cannot for sure or for long, what other people think of them. They are afraid to find out, so cast about for many and various validators of their status. Social media platforms thrive on "a new kind of psyche that seeks, through its exposed virtual self, satisfactions of approval and notoriety that it can never truly find" (Bernard Harcourt). "Players" escape social isolation only to find themselves in a digital prison and solitary confinement. The effect is more not less alienation, loss of both self-direction and connection with other people. "Dancing With the Stars" attracts minor-celebrity contestants—some of them White House castoffs, in whose self-demeaning antics Trump must take savage delight—who work their literal butts off in order to stay noticed. In conjunction with televised professional sport, the other games some people play affect everybody, because sport and entertainment are no longer niche economies but a single industry that increasingly dictates how every other product, service and "property" (including human beings) is marketed.

Society's crush of anonymity makes people want to be noticed—or not unnoticed. The double negative suggests a less than wholehearted pursuit of notice. Being noticed can be publicly embarrassing, even humiliating. Nowadays, with CCTV surveillance of more and more public space, a surreptitious crotch scratch can end up on the Internet, and be interpreted as proof of sexual deviance. No one wants that kind of notice. But is that entirely true? The notorious fact that the most intimate, cringe-inducing details of a person's private life, wishfully assumed to be only for the eyes and ears of a select one or few, are, once electronically posted, ultimately available to the whole world doesn't seem to stop some people seeking notice at any cost. Rousseau's reservations have been cast aside. The craving for mass respect is a self-destructive self-contradiction that cancels concern about disrespect for persons and loss of human dignity. Mass murder is one way for the disappointed seeker for distinction, from the mass and by the mass, to compensate for his or her failure: give "them" something to remember "me" by. And one of the goals of many mass murderers is suicide—to kill the self that stares back at them in the mocking mirror of fame. This can be the end game of attention-seeking. It was not the goal of Albert Camus' outsider Meursault awaiting execution. Like him, but more absurdly than stoically, the lonely attention-seeker can look forward, in grim satisfaction or anticipatory gratification, to public "howls of execration."

· · · · ·

Life in an acquisitive society generates an unquenchable thirst for fame. Hobbes recognized this peculiarly human need, this ambition, as a form of lust for power, power for its own sake and as a means to acquire more property and thereby more power—and fame. Locke said personal property includes life and liberty, as a precondition for acquiring land and material possessions. Each in its own way could be said to be a matter of personal presence and standing in society, and as a way of asserting oneself against it or in contradistinction to it—making them more public than private matters. Acquisitiveness (or what C.B. Macpherson termed possessive individualism) is about status (however fleeting compared to its older meaning, estate), repute (ill or otherwise), and the attention attracted by great wealth, inherited or self-amassed, as much as it is about the money, land and other possessions themselves. In life as in death, a wealthy recluse is a target for feverish speculation, interest in the person a match for the interest on his or her wealth. If they are not reclusive, wealthy people are bound to display their wealth in some way or other, however discreetly. Some flaunt it, and most of them who use the power it gives them behind the scenes, in the political wings, do not retreat from view when they are uncovered.

The Koch, Mellon and other lesser-known American billionaire families have, until quite recently, kept their political philanthropy veiled, funding purportedly non-partisan think tanks legally permitted to spend up to 50% of their money on political action, most of it anti-regulation and anti-taxation. Electoral success has emboldened the founders of such family "public service" foundations. Charles Koch, a generous contributor to the arts, used the occasion of his donating his money (and his name) to a museum to archly allude to the Koch dynasty's other, political good works. In response to evidence and criticism that their foundation for world public health was making money from pollution-heavy industries, co-chairs Bill and Melinda Gates decided to continue their investment in them and rely on investor voting to influence those industries' policy and conduct. How many shareholders actually go to meetings and voice support for board candidates or motions not recommended by the corporation's directors; or, a little less unlikely, vote by proxy ballot? Two compensating things can be said. First, some rare fireworks can occur when a corporation's leadership is personally challenged from the floor and the press reports it. Second, close interaction with public health professionals on the board of the Gates foundation made it possible for Bill to warn, in a 2015 Ted Talk, about much of exactly what has happened in the 2020 Covid-19 pandemic.

The "legions" of Anonymous (a group self-identifying as anarchist, and opposed to both state power and private wealth concentration) are not truly anonymous, even when they don masks in public. One of them can be seen, in a photo of the 2013 "Million Mask March" in Washington, D.C., lifting his mask, peeking out, looking around as if to see who and how many are looking at him.

— CHAPTER 20 —

General Will and Private Self

The remedy for succumbing to conspicuous consumption's blandishments, and for self-defeating (in both senses of the word) psychic dependence on others, is political participation with them. It might be called a continuing soulful political education—Rousseau's "paradoxical and anguished thought…scrutinized his memory in a constant quest for the affective shock that took the place of religion" (Julia Kristeva). Being aspirational, his idea of a social contract was bound to conflict with many political realities, some of which he wrote into his theorizing, as if acutely conscious that some of it would be a hard sell. *Du Contrat social* opens with a familiar quotation: "Man was born free, and he is everywhere in chains." The second sentence is less lapidary, and heavy with a rich future harvest of philosophical progeny: "Those who think themselves the masters of others are indeed greater slaves than they." Heirs include Hegel's dialectic of master and slave and the multi-faceted theory of alienation. The next lines hint at uncertainty and portend buyer's remorse: "How did this transformation come about? I do not know. How can it be made [to look? to feel?] legitimate? That question I believe I can answer."

His hypothetical way out of the predicament of personal identity loss leading to social alienation raises the bar for moral courage, takes it to a different place: beyond standing alone against a corrupt society to exercising one's political will as an expression of one's *moi commun*. It has been called the voice of social conscience, continually rediscovered and reactivated through one's political participation or community service. In life as a communal being "I" am what "my" better self (angel?) expects of me. This is a stern directive, one that has to be freely self-initiated and self-imposed. But as he so (in)famously said, the general or collective will can force people to be free, autonomous moral beings. This paradox is grounded in a people's unanimous agreement that they have a general will; for them to have a political order at all, each and every person must—logically, not actually—be a party to its founding social contract. As with some other democracy theorists, his "working" model was a hypothetical community of independent, self-sufficient farmers and artisans made even more equal by being citizen-soldiers (the quasi-mythic classical republic and face-to-face society). His native city of Geneva had some of that quality, in part due to its Calvinist ethos, which also played a part in his decision to self-deport to France, Catholicism and older women of means—while fathering five children with his long-suffering "companion" Thérèse Le Vasseur, whose occupation, luckily for him, was laundress.

Political decisions made, and laws enacted, will probably all be by majority vote of some kind, and individual votes may be based on a partial or factional interest, or on an entirely personal one. "Even in selling his vote for money, he [an elector or an elected representative] does not extinguish the general will in himself; he evades it." Establishing that there is a general will or overriding public interest is one thing; acting on it, another. "For this reason the sensible rule for regulating public assemblies is one intended not so much to uphold the general will there as to ensure that it is always questioned and always responds"

(Rousseau, *The Social Contract*, trans. Maurice Cranston, Book IV, ch. 1, "That the General Will is Indestructible").

Scottish Enlightenment figures Adam Ferguson, John Millar and Adam Smith—and American Founding Fathers who knew their work—believed that moral self-discipline, not necessarily dependent on religious sanctions, is needed to contain the social forces and ambitions that human ingenuity and passion have unleashed. They sought (from their various perspectives) the cure for these ills in study of their causes—as did Rousseau. Advocates for Adam Smith's laissez-faire (hands-off) model of a free-market economy tend to ignore or downplay his work on "moral sentiments" and the role of self-restraint, of a self-installed judge or censor, in all our social relations. The American philosopher and jurist Ronald Dworkin has argued that "an impartial, objective attitude toward all citizens" is a principle independent of societal facts, and unaffected by denial of theoretically inconvenient ones. It is an ethics proposition about moral sense and moral judgment, like Kant's categorical imperative, and open to argument only on those grounds. Peter Singer—called a Nazi (as in *Seinfeld*'s "Soup Nazi"?) by some commentators on account of his "extreme" moral strictures, an extreme reaction to his views that he shares with Rousseau—says "radical impartiality will make us individually happy by giving meaning to our lives." For Singer, radical impartiality means *all* animals being treated with the same respect.

They were thinking more of classical writers on republican virtue than of French Enlightenment figures, and certainly not of Rousseau, but the American "Framers" were akin to him in their idea of civic virtue and its intellectual, and martial, ancestry. Rousseau had a fondness for lawgivers in the classical mould, especially for those seen as "fathers" of nations being born or imagined in his own day—and who were also heroes of armed liberation, such as George Washington and Pasquale

Paoli of Corsica (for which "nation" both he and Rousseau wrote constitutions). In one of his "confessions" Rousseau says: "I had come to see that everything was radically connected with politics and that whatever was done about it, no nation would be other than what the nature of its government made it." While the "Legislator" may be a godlike moulder of men, a good code of basic laws needs good citizens willing to act in its spirit.

Protecting and preserving the U.S. constitution against extreme factionalism and self-interest requires more than institutional checks and balances and anti-bribery laws. The citizenry as a whole must act as citizens. And that means more than lobbying, petitioning and voting; it means an enduring moral commitment to the public interest. In James Madison's words: "To suppose that any form of government will secure liberty or happiness without any virtue in the people is a chimerical idea." He was not referring to people refraining from fornication or their tithing a church; he was talking about public political virtue—which is what Rousseau's general will is all about. It is ideologically misrepresented as a disguise for despot-imposed diktat; whereas it is the idea of a self-directed individual will to achieve, with other such wills, the common good. In practice, says Rousseau, it usually means majority rule, and obedience to laws that others have made and that you and/or I do not entirely agree with. That obedience is based on acceptance of the underlying rightness of the system that produces those laws and political decisions.

That kind of obedience sounds like Canadian political deference, encapsulated in our Christmas-cracker motto, "Peace, order and good government"—in contrast to the high-flying American one, "Life, liberty and the pursuit of happiness." They may be more alike than they appear. Substitute "felicity" for "happiness" and one could arrive at the felicific calculus, which Thomas Jefferson, an avid reader of books by

Enlightenment figures, may have encountered. Whatever he may or may not have read, Jefferson may have known of the Hobbesian idea that one's felicity depends on it being compared to others'—and envied by them. So at least one American Framer may have conceived of happiness in quasi-communitarian as well as libertarian terms; maybe he was also thinking of human equality (as in "all men are created equal") and even of "the greatest happiness of the greatest number."

. . . . .

The triple blow of pandemic, economic recession and the culminating exposure of systemic racism has made the American dream look more like a guttering bedside candle than a hilltop beacon of light. Mask-wearing and self-quarantine are contrary to the American spirit, making it easy for President Trump to incite resistance to public health pleas for collective self-discipline and community co-operation. His rhetoric may sound expansive, but the substance of his message is contraction—behind immigration walls and tariff barriers, without any international obligations. Marilynne Robinson says that Americans "should step away from the habit of accepting competition as the basic model of our interactions with other countries"—and with each other—and that "recent history has shown that the adversary is actually us"—which was pointed out 65 years ago by Walt Kelly's "Pogo."

She also writes liberally (as in a combination of the first five OED meanings of the word "liberal") about an American humanist heritage in public higher education; and about the growing *verkrampte* grip of cost-benefit analysis on all learning and scholarship. This has been for the singular benefit of the business and technology leaders produced by (the product of?) advanced education, and at the cost of an impoverished industrial precariat—as it's now known; she also remarks on the strange persistence of some Marxian categories in the theory and practice of what German sociologist Wolfgang Streeck calls "senescent" neo-liberal capitalism. He says that "compared to economic relations, political relations are…by necessity rigid and persistent; they emphasize strong ties of duty rather than weak ties of choice. They are obligatory rather than voluntary… demanding sacrifices in utility and effort; and they insist on loyalty." Against the "weak" freedom of choice in a market cornucopia—labelled scarcity in order to justify austerity for the masses, says Robinson—"the role of citizen requires a disciplined readiness to accept decisions that one had originally opposed, or that are contrary to one's interests" (*How Will Capitalism End?*, 2016, pp. 107-08). Could Streeck be referring to Robinson's (temporarily) lost American values? Loyalty? To what? Josiah Royce's "community of interpretations"? His so-called objective idealism, a neo-Hegelian stew of rational will, absolute truth and the marriage of earthly and divine love, was puckishly portentous, an embrace that could stretch to include Trump's smarmy cuddling of the American flag. Oh well, Royce was from California.

Neither a chastened Rousseauian social contract nor a neo-Marxian *Kulturkampf* can help explain, let alone resolve, the American political tragedy. Once again, we must consult the poets. Here's D.H. Lawrence on Herman Melville, author of the American Bible, *Moby Dick*.

> What then is Moby Dick? He is the deepest blood-being of the white race; he is our deepest blood-nature.
> And he is hunted, hunted, hunted by the maniacal fanaticism of our white mental consciousness. We want to hunt him down. To subject him to our will. And in this maniacal conscious hunt of ourselves we get dark races and pale to help us, red, yellow and black, east and west, Quaker and fire-worshiper, we get them all to help us in this ghastly maniacal hunt which is our doom and our suicide.

The last phallic being of the white man. Hunted into the death of upper consciousness and the ideal will. Our blood-self subjected to our will. Our blood-consciousness sapped by a parasitic mental or ideal consciousness.

If the Great White Whale sank the ship of the Great White Soul in 1851, what's been happening ever since?

Post-mortem effects, presumably.

One of these was Walt Whitman, and "his message of American democracy."

Purified of MERGING, purified of MYSELF, the exultant message of American Democracy, of souls in the Open Road, full of glad recognition, full of fierce readiness, full of the joy of worship, when one soul sees a greater soul.

(Edmund Wilson, *The Shock of Recognition*, 1943, pp. 1060-61 and 1077)

Melville and Whitman died in 1891 and 1892; Royce in 1916; and Lawrence in 1930. So what happened since then—other than the U.S. replacing the U.K. as world pax master and the oceans becoming a cesspool? In America, there has been a lot of breast-beating, as Abraham Lincoln's emancipation of Confederacy slaves turned into a more bitter and long-drawn-out disappointment for the emancipated than the contemporaneous emancipation of Russian serfs by Alexander II.

Getting back to Donald Trump, with whom the preceding excursion into American history and literature began, he has difficulty dealing with smart women, many of whom are journalists, which doubles his vexation. His bête noire, Speaker of the House Nancy Pelosi, has decided to ignore him, which upsets his ego more than her contempt for him. The Governor of Michigan is "that woman." Justin Trudeau, a self-proclaimed feminist, was expected to be an urbane Prime Minister, thus provoking a belligerent Leader of the Opposition into faux pas (a reciprocal aim). Early in his PM career, Justin, former nightclub bouncer, decided to take the lead in breaking up what looked like a brawl in the aisle between government and opposition benches in the House of Commons. His well-intentioned intervention—and we know what happens to good intentions—resulted in his bumping into a gentle-woman NDP MP from Quebec. His apology to the Speaker did not quell cries of "Arrogance!" and "Assault!"—and, of course, "Resign!" This incident marred the popular image of a Prime Minister with a gender-balanced cabinet.

Shades of current Ontario Premier Doug Ford's brother Rob, who, when mayor of Toronto, ran into an elderly lady councillor—on foot, during a council meeting, not in his Hummer—which amazed U.S. viewers of another in a series of vignettes of Canadian political rough-and-tumble. There seems to be a subliminal Canadian longing for politics to be played like the national sport, dominated by players who prefer to heavily board their opponents rather than skate circles around them. It's all good clean horse (or Moosehead) play. Being one of the lads is less about being a womanizer and *bon vivant* than a slightly concussed (even stupefied) good fellow. Heavy-drinking leaders were long felt acceptable, as well as male chauvinists. But no sexual violence, please—two former Premiers, of Nova Scotia and Saskatchewan, ran afoul of that unwritten rule. You stand some chance of being forgiven a drunk-driving conviction, not one for sexual assault. Former B.C. Premier Gordon Campbell suffered no lasting political damage from a DUI on Maui and a widely circulated mug shot—he was obviously led astray by the devil-may-care American lifestyle.

· · · · ·

In "Lame Shadows, " which first appeared in the *New York Review of Books* in 1970, three years before his death, W.H. Auden attacked artists who took themselves too seriously—and their patrons, who found it difficult to take seriously the dignity of those "whose lives their wealth and power do so much to determine."

> Community still means what it always has, a group of persons united by love of something other than themselves...such a love has to be discovered by each person for himself; it cannot be acquired socially.
> Society can only teach conformity to the momentary fashion, either of the majority or of its mirror image, the rebellious minority. Today, all visible and therefore social signs of agreement are suspect.

As a critic of society's artistic (and other) fashions, Rousseau would probably have agreed with Auden; and one would like to think he could see himself reflected in the mirror of fashionable rebellion. Auden seems to have shared Rousseau's longing for something solid beneath the social surface that would strengthen the unity in "community." Also like Rousseau, he saw the proliferation of social distinctions as a sign of society's failure to help all manner of persons create a moral core sustained by an independent character. If there are no teaching examples of the *moi commun* and everyone has to find community for himself or herself alone, there will be, Auden says, no great society, only a big one full of self-absorbed individuals.

In the absence of a well-developed political culture of civic virtue and a widespread sense of *moi commun*, a person could reasonably (if somewhat fatalistically) fall back on neo-Stoic *amour de soi*—become a "solitary [but not totally anti-social] walker" free-associating in his "reveries" (Thoreau on Walden Pond, of whom it has been said that he regularly left Walden for the suburban comforts of the Boston family home). Or one could embrace what metaphysician John McDowell calls "undogmatic quietism," associated with the "consolations of philosophy" tradition. A similar alternative to the everyday, unsung heroism of political battle is something American short-story writer J.F. Powers put in the mouth of one of his retiring (but not yet retired) priest characters, in a story entitled "Zeal": "He wanted to say that he believed people should do what they could do, little though it might be, and shouldn't be asked to attempt what was obviously beyond them." These are neither doctrines nor postures, nor bystander attitudes of say-nothing, do-nothing. Life is full of occasions that call for decisive action. Just don't beat yourself up when your best efforts turn out badly; you'll get enough of that from officious others.

— CHAPTER 21 —

Clôture

Clôture comes, as the circumflex over the "o" indicates, from France, where it originated as a motion to terminate debate. It has been adopted elsewhere—e.g., in Australia, where it is (fittingly) called the guillotine. It's cloture (no diacritical mark) in the U.K. and the U.S., where it is mostly known as a motion to end a filibuster in the Senate. Closure of debate in the B.C. House is provided for in standing order 46. Calling it closure suggests an affinity with the hope, now increasingly a demand, that difficult matters be resolved in such a way that all concerned can say they're satisfied the "issue" has been filed free of any unanswered questions or ill will. If the Chair finds it neither premature nor an infringement of members' rights, the following motion to immediately move to a vote on the motion under debate is put to a vote without debate or amendment: "That the question be now put." It's safe to assume its passage, and of whatever it was the government felt it was past time to dispose of and get on with its agenda; but the substance of the "question" (not the closure motion as such) may later be "renewed." The 1983 "endless summer" session in B.C.'s legislature ended October 21, when closure was used to pass all the government's fiscal-restraint bills. Closure was first mooted on September 26 by John (Richard III) Reynolds, chief executioner when it was finally time to call time on weeks of round-the-clock sittings (with weekends off)—"Now is the summer of our discontent made glorious autumn." It was all provoked by the government challenging opposition members' oratorical capacity by refusing to adjourn debate.

The following bit of B.C. legislative debate occurred during a sitting of the House in Committee of Supply on April 28, 1989. The occasion was estimates of the Attorney-General ministry—supply of its budgetary allowance for the next fiscal year, after opposition inquiry into how well (or not) the minister spent the previous one.

> Today I want to bring to the Attorney-General the concern that I believe is out there in the community for the compassion for this tiny, defenceless, vulnerable child—in many cases, an infant.
>
> I frankly believe that we have a responsibility in this House to bring that concern to the attention of the community. That's why we were elected; that's why we sit in this chamber. Today I want to speak for those children, and I want to speak for all of the people in the community who are, quite frankly, outraged by every case they read about.
>
> But I wanted, just frankly, to get the opinion of the Attorney-General and to get the feeling of the House, and the outrage of the community, when this kind of sentencing is given—this light sentencing for murder. I want to put it on the record. I feel strongly, as a parent and a citizen, as a British Columbian, that I speak on behalf of people who read of these cases, week in, week out—and they have no criticism of our judicial system, Mr.Chairman; nor do I.

> Sometimes I think we have to remind the people in
> the judiciary, whom we entrust to do that balance of
> compassion and responsibility, of what the community
> is thinking. We have to catch them up a bit, maybe, on
> where we are today.

The speaker was Grace McCarthy, at that time the first member for Vancouver—Little Mountain. For many years she had held high office in a succession of Social Credit governments, including the post of Deputy Premier. She had (or been) retired to the government back benches because of animosity between her and the man who in 1986 "stole" the reward due her for decades of party and public service: leader of the Social Credit Party and the post of Premier. I remember seeing Bill Reid, Vander Zalm's Minister of Tourism, but more courtier than cabinet minister, bursting from the shotgun seat of the Premier's Crown Victoria, bounding back up the steps to the Premier's office, and returning seconds later with what looked like a potted plant, which he placed in the king's hand hanging languidly from the royal coach's right rear window. (Reid was one of the Zalm's Surrey municipal politics cronies, and best-known for shouting, when still a back-bencher, "That's leadership, that's good government," whenever any Socred minister stood up in the House to speak.) The plant he handed to his boss was probably a poinsettia, apt symbol of the poisonous relationship between Vander Zalm and McCarthy. A florist by profession, she delivered flower arrangements to all legislative offices every Christmas. She was a walking, talking Hallmark greeting card, also notable for her Smile campaign, her own being in the mouth but not in the eyes.

The Attorney-General was Stuart "Bud" Smith, who had replaced Brian Smith, the next speaker in the debate, as A-G. Brian made some lawyerly comments on certain areas of responsibility in the A-G ministry, ignoring Grace's unlawyerly attack on the judiciary. He came second, ahead of Grace, at the 1986 convention that created Premier Bill Vander Zalm, and was in the process of baling out of the sinking Socred ship. "Bud" was enjoying his important cabinet post, but mindful of the deference due such a party stalwart as Grace, who was a protégé of B.C. Social Credit Party founder W.A.C. Bennett and herself a Socred icon. In reply to her veiled attack on his administration of his ministry, he spent more words acknowledging Grace's great work as a former Minister of Human Resources, the value of her comments, and how much he shared her outrage, than he did on a standard defence of ministry (including judicial) conduct and the great progress made under his leadership.

When a politician repeatedly says that she is speaking frankly, it may be a speech tic. However, whether subconscious or not and regardless of the process whereby it might have become subconscious, it arouses suspicion that there is something else going on, that there is less than full disclosure. McCarthy was getting her licks in at, putting her street cred to, a government that, without her in charge, was losing touch with the electorate. The redundant "frankly"s were not otiose. They added to a knowledgeable listener's or reader's appreciation of her tortured articulation of personal political anger, disguised as giving voice to community outrage at an injustice: against a "vulnerable child," Grace McCarthy, the dowager duchess if not the queen of the Social Credit Party, a woman in politics….

She recounted half a dozen "sensational" cases, including one of a shaken baby who died. Serious doubts have since been raised about many of the guilty verdicts involving shaken-baby syndrome. But MLAs continue to avail themselves of their lofty public platform, and of parliamentary privilege, to re-try these and similar cases and to re-sentence the defendants. McCarthy asserted that two years for manslaughter (increased to four on appeal) was too light for murder (her word). Admittedly, the case was closed, no longer *sub judice*. But second-guessing the court and inciting lynch-mob-like sentiments do nothing for the dignity of the House. To claim that conveying her constituents' heartfelt feelings was her duty as their elected representative is insufficient justification for her performance on this occasion. Perhaps we should ring-fence this lapse from Grace in a long legislative career with a cloture, which can also mean protective fencing, often made more attractive by artfully attached or planted greenery and by floral displays.

· · · · ·

The rules, or conventions, about permissible or appropriate subjects of debate are not applied consistently—the only consistency is in the use of standing orders to defer or curtail debate if the government so wishes. It is not entirely clear what the rules have to say, or what they direct, in all circumstances—especially in a committee hearing, where junior Clerks are likely to be the ones advising the Chair. After hearing a detailed account of a case of Munchausen's syndrome, with proper names, a B.C. select standing committee decided to order all words about the case "expunged" from the record on grounds of doctor-patient confidentiality. This sensitivity tardiness meant that the public gallery, which contained journalists, heard all the offending words. Today they would have been publicly audio-streamed in real time; some of them might have appeared as a hypertext first draft, as Blues on the Net—there's a title for a Hansard theme song. They were not, as we are often told today, redacted (visibly blacked out). Human memory aside, there is no hard evidence for this episode. Any paper trail was trashed or recycled long ago; the audiotapes were erased, reused and finally disposed of as unusable. I asked my Ontario counterpart about debate-expunging. He told me he had never heard of, let alone encountered, anything like it.

It is of particular interest that this apparently unique (in a Canadian legislature) case of words forbidden after the fact of their utterance was about a mother who had been diagnosed with Munchausen's by proxy. A person with this syndrome projects a complaint or grievance onto another person, often the subject's own child, in an attempt to excite sympathy and get special treatment for a supposed affliction or injury. It takes hypochondria to a level beyond Molière's *malade imaginaire*, who is not seriously ill but sincerely believes he (or she) is. Munchausen's is a morbid condition. Its victims tell tall tales about themselves and their lives, including tragic mishaps and heroic mistakes. Freiherr von Münchhausen was a real person who led an adventurous life; but his most extravagant exploits were concocted later by Rudolf Raspe in *Baron Munchausen's Travels and Campaigns in Russia*. The baron himself (or his "good name"?) became an eponym because of a fabulist's fiction. It could be said that his reputation became the victim of Munchausen's "victims." The quasi-imaginary quality of what people with this syndrome say does not make it spurious: psychosomatic (mind-body) illnesses are by no means entirely unreal. In Munchausen's, the line between real and fake illness is difficult to discern.

In its proxy form, a surrogate is used to attract sympathetic attention and divert or dilute disbelief. A minor or someone else not equipped to fully grasp what is going on—and powerless to do anything about it—is the preferred object of the subject, and is made into a kind of ventriloquist's dummy. People with Munchausen's "enjoy" the ambivalence of suffering from a set of disease symptoms and acting them out in a way that appears to be free of any dependency; ventriloquists have admitted to a similar bifurcation. Munchausen's-by-proxy subjects have difficulty distinguishing between themselves and the object(s) of their manipulation.

One might think that Munchausen's "patients" would exhibit psychic agitation. But their belief that their medical history is entirely factual is unshakeable; and as with the brave baron's adventures, there is an allegedly reliable third party, or a proxy, who will so attest. Robert Ripley of "Ripley's Believe It or Not" confidently stated that all the natural wonders in his "odditorium" had been verified as non-fakes by his trusty assistants. Of course, that's easy to do when you live in Hollywood, land of make-believe, where there is no need to fight off scoffers and skeptics—they always play along. But anywhere will do. The "patient" patiently, calmly hawks his or her story from doctor to doctor, from clinic to hospital, from politician to press—to anyone who will listen. The only true Munchausen's sufferers are those on the receiving end. They are at a disadvantage because the "victim" has support(ers); the listeners, whatever and however strong their doubts, are either inclined or duty-bound (or both) to give him or her a full and attentive hearing.

One doesn't have to delve deeply into this syndrome to find affinities with some sorts of political pathology—and a (perhaps subconscious) motive for wanting to stop any further consideration of Munchausen's by the aforementioned committee. Members may have sensed an uncomfortable closeness to such phenomena as:

- elected representatives' identification with constituents and constituencies that can turn into a mutual appropriation;
- self-promotion "forced" on candidates by party and constituency associations but feigned reluctance to be anything other than their constituents' "humble servant";
- finger-pointing evasion of the elected ones' accountability for misconduct followed by a sense of entitlement to full forgiveness and re-election;
- inability of governed and governors to speak truth to one another, only sullen rancour from the former and blatant flattery from the latter.

That's the "good stuff" promising spicy moral hazard, exciting opportunities for young interns, and grim satisfaction for old observers. The truly good stuff is full of decency and diligence, the meat and potatoes of political life. Remove references to democratic politics from the above list, and it reads like a slice of everyday life. Is Munchausen's one of those theories that convert normal human experience into a lucrative mental illness field for professional (or not) therapists and counsellors?

There is now Munchausen's by Internet. Some people who create, and "curate," online self-profiles say they have Munchausen's, and describe themselves as multiply afflicted—with serious physical injuries, a wasting or otherwise terminal illness, and at least one recently deceased family member. Unfortunately for their efforts to gain viral sympathy, a few who have seen these accounts (with pictures of the sufferers) have been moved to investigate the truth of what was being broadcast; in some cases money had changed hands. One result has been a veritable industry devoted to the exposure of lies, prompting (as so often happens on the Net) vengeful attacks on "scam artists" followed by the same on those who exposed them. Some retribution was not virtual but real. People who communicate only by electronic means find it hard to know what a flesh-and-blood person is.

• • • • •

In the final subsection of Michael Oakeshott's introduction to *Leviathan*, "Beyond Politics," he quotes an ancient Chinese sage: when there is no water and "the fish are all together on dry land" they will "keep each other wet with their slime. But this is not to be compared with their forgetting each other in a river or a lake." Our wireless wired world is an illusion of togetherness within a dream of forgetfulness, where there is no salve in virtual slime, no power to comfort or heal. Entering the sixth (and by no means the final) month of our isolated and anxious dependence on electronic (or just telephonic) communication, we wonder what lasting damage might have been done to all manner of human relationships when the "divine wind" of Covid-19 passes on—only to be replaced by another mutant, novel coronavirus.

From another poetical perspective, one that reminds us of our place in a natural world that relates to us but is essentially indifferent to us, comes a reflection on forgetting "the lives we've imagined as we carry the lives we have [and] all the lives we have lost...." It rests on a close encounter with a member of the other class of non-human animals that live primarily in another element, air not water in this case.

> I wish that we would not fight for landscapes that remind us of who we think we are. I wish, instead, for landscapes buzzing and glowing with life in all its variousness. And I am guilty too. I'd wanted to escape history by running to the hawk...but my flight was wrong. Worse than wrong. It was dangerous. *I must fight, always, against forgetting*, I thought.
> (Helen Macdonald, *H is for Hawk*, 2014, p. 265.)

This is somewhat ambiguous: maybe "I thought" wrong. Our self-consciousness and its memories are often thought to be enervating. We believe that other animals are blessed with nothing they have to forget—no worries about other "lives lost." We're a bit amphibian, which means being a bit reptilian, living in a watery and an airy world. Robert Macfarlane's *Underland: A Deep Time Journey* reminds us of our subterranean lives, our hidden history. It would slow us down—not necessarily a bad thing—but the occasional longer look in the rear-view mirror (are objects still closer than they appear?), requiring less forward speed for safety's sake, would be a good thing. The past can rush up from way back, and from below, returning to bite us in the backside.

— APPENDICES —

Pre-Traumatic Stress Disorder

Birth is a trauma. But it marks the beginning of life, which is generally considered a good thing. Part of living is the experience of traumas, if not, as some say they experience, one uninterrupted trauma. People born into wealth and its comforts are protected from many of the traumas that others experience. Even if they have sibling competition or mix with other (perhaps resentful, less-advantaged) children, their own family life and inheritance tends to ensure an easy self-confidence.

Many countries copy the British practice of sending upper-class offspring to private (in England, public) schools or academies of instruction in military discipline and good manners. This experience, depending in part on its duration, may temper childish egocentricity. For most people, the schoolyard "games" of socialization are a physically and emotionally testing experience, one tending to induce a wary respect for others. And exchange of blows and insults gives way to displays of wit.

A lesson learned by bullies is that they can get what they want more easily by being overbearing rather than merely belligerent. Some combine their dominating nature and nurture to create a formidable presence, and use it to build a succession of successes, layer upon layer. The news of each successive layer is spread by people who, as usual and allowing for the usual embellishments, want the gist of their reports believed. From its creator to its converts, the story is made "to be believed"—make-believe, one might say.

How far can this be made to go? What is any one person's pinnacle of desire? It may be enough to be a Don Juan, with a belt full of sexual-conquest notches; and/or a multi-billionaire, but not a miser or recluse; above all, a celebrity, known for being known, even if it's primarily because of a talent for self-promotion.

Here hubris creeps into the daily pace of personal ambition. Is there some high attainment requiring little or no effort to keep attention focused on oneself, a place that is a magnet for attention and cynosure of admiration? On such a stage the light is going to be very bright and very hot. It could be likened to a kitchen. DJ finds he has to beat his wings faster and faster to stay lit up—it's hard to keep it up. Thanks to breeding and luck, and a following of true believers, he has led a trauma-free life. Unprepared for the stress of attaining what he thought was his heart's desire, he cannot control the unfamiliar disorder that he helped create and is destroying him.

If only he'd been put in the care of a governess from an early age, one who would have regularly pulled down his pants and smacked his saucy bare bottom.

The New-Old Time Machine

> AND a young stud at the next table typing on his laptop, both ears stopped with earphones. I'm just five feet from the guy. Finally I say in a friendly voice, "You from around here? Haven't seen you before in the

neighborhood." No answer. He continues typing, staring at the laptop. He heard nothing? Is this body alive? I'm alarmed. I call 911. After some time a cop car arrives and he's arrested for "non-participation in human-ity." They haul the corpse away.

Lawrence Ferlinghetti (100)

I enter the elevator. There are three other people—this is before the pandemic. Across from me a young woman is looking and pointing some-thing at me. She says: "You doing anything tonight?" She must be talking to the younger guy beside me. I look at him. He shrugs. So I say: "No. How about you?" She giggles nervously. Older woman looks vaguely alarmed. Younger guy: "She's talking on her phone." He and I get off at our floor. "It's a crazy world," he says. I have to agree.

Peter Robbins (80)

The eloi came out of the great 2020 pandemic unscathed. They don't actually come out of doors much. They stay in electronic communicado with other eloi. They order what they need, or want, wirelessly, through e-mail, e-hail, e-bail and e-tail. For the last two or three they may have to mix with the polloi, who live outside mostly, on mostly empty streets. Or in parks, hiding from eloi expeditions. Eloi wear viewing machines on their heads, which they say enhances what they visualize. They don't understand when asked what they see. One side effect of the so-called Chinese virus was losing the sense of smell. Living inside, in super-san-itized rooms, can't help. The polloi live in the dark a lot, which means a lot of smelling your way around. They hear things too. So do the eloi, but electronically "enhanced."

Dogs' sense of smell wasn't affected by the virus. When they're walking with their owners, it's that old joke about who's walking whom—the polloi still talk like that. One guy was seen following his dog's nose ac-ross a street without looking. Not that streets are very busy these days. But he followed the dog through some bushes and back across the street. This time he almost collided with one of those silent Teslas.

The polloi keep on sniffing, searching for the scent of old memories. Some use old cell phones to hack into the eloi network—if they can find batteries. All kinds of stuff is advertised online, but nobody inside accepts cash anymore. The most finely tuned noses can snuffle-truffle many useful things. Like cans of dog food—which has long been better than a lot of what humans eat—and eloi waste that isn't garbage. The polloi hijack food trucks of various kinds. They better be careful: eloi surveillance drones are being armed. War of the worlds…to be continued.